WHAT LEADERS ARE SAYING ABOUT DISCOVER THE JOY OF LEADERSHIP

This book is a wonderful reflection on the breadth of Willy's insightful counsel that he has provided to me and many of my leadership team over the years. I trust you will benefit as we have.
—Paul E. Purcell, Chairman, Robert W. Baird & Co., Inc. For 13 years, Baird has been honored among FORTUNE's 100 Best Companies to Work For.®

Willy Steiner is a leadership master. When I was running a large organization and needed an experienced hand to work with my executives, Willy was always who I would call for help. He helped me handle a variety of managers with a variety of issues and was effective in getting all of them moving in the right direction and actually changing and recognizing their behavior. This book is the "how to" handbook on Leadership. Anyone who considers themselves a leader at any level should have this book in their library…and USE IT.
—Rita Schaefer, Publishing Executive.

What a great gift to have Willy Steiner's succinct and savvy guide to leadership. As my executive coach, Willy always brought nuance and perspective to our discussions. He excels in the art of "sensemaking"—listening carefully to his clients, helping them interpret their dilemmas, and suggesting paths they might consider. His advice was consistently wise and thoughtful, and I could not have asked for a better partner.
—John Pauly, Provost, Marquette University, 2008-13 and currently "Gretchen and Cyril Colnik Chair in Communication, Marquette University."

Over the years, I have appreciated Willy's direct and well-informed approach to providing suggestions and insights. For those who take advantage of its counsel, this book should prove to be an invaluable resource for both an organization's leaders and their teams.

—Paul J. Carbone, Managing Partner, Pritzker Group Private Capital

Willy showed me, and many on my team over the years, a path to becoming a much more effective manager. As my roles and responsibilities grew over the years, this foundation helped me in becoming a good leader as well. I am sure that Discover the Joy of Leadership can assist you in your personal leadership journey as well.

—Todd Dolan, Group Vice President, Software Development, Charter Communications

Early in my career, Coach Willy provided me with the no-nonsense counsel I need to adapt successfully to a broader leadership role. I trust that Discover the Joy of Leadership can assist you in a similar manner.

—Harley J. Goldstein, Esq., Founding Partner & Chairman, Goldstein & McClintock LLLP

DISCOVER THE JOY
OF LEADERSHIP

DISCOVER THE JOY OF LEADERSHIP

A Practical Guide to Resolving Your Management Challenges

WILLIAM G. STEINER

ECC Publishing

978-0-9969577-0-0 (paperback)
978-0-9969577-1-7 (mobi)
978-0-9969577-2-4 (ePub)

LCCN: 2016953876

Cover Design by Willy Steiner
Cover art by Sarah Zeffiro, zeffiroart.com

DEDICATION

IT HAS BEEN MY HONOR AND PLEASURE to have served so many leaders over the years and I have learned from every one of you. This book is dedicated to all those who have ever had the courage to step up and lead a team, a group or even a company. Some get to such a position by choice, design or the result of concerted effort to learn and grow into it. Others often land there by default, either by being in the right place at the right time or seeing a need to marshal the forces of others to a common goal or purpose and doing their best to make that happen. Leading can be very rewarding but it is often very frustrating, made difficult by the conflicting needs and ideas of the many and the complexity of being human.

The age-old question of whether leaders are born or made is not one I will take a position on. But I hope that some of the thoughts, ideas and models I have presented here will assist anyone who has chosen to take up this daunting challenge of leading others. I trust you will gain insights and suggestions for actions that will assist you, your team and your organization. I have the greatest respect for anyone who willingly takes on this task.

This book is also dedicated to the memory of Jim Coar, my mentor during my early career at the RCA Corporation. Jim believed in and challenged me and opened my mind to the need for and process of developing leaders. It has been a focus of my intellectual development and a passion of mine ever since. He would be proud of what I have done with my coaching career and service to others. He was a model for me. He also became a wonderful friend and I do miss him.

CONTENTS

TIME

COMMUNICATION

INTRODUCTION

I SAW THIS QUOTATION recently and it reminded me of why I've been able to be in business as an executive leadership coach for almost 20 years:

CFO to the CEO: What happens if we spend training funds developing our people and then they leave us?

CEO to CFO: What happens if we don't and they stay?

Here's a little background (I promise, just a little) to provide perspective. Early in my career I was fortunate to work in the leadership development functions of two major corporations, the RCA Corporation and General Electric. The RCA Corporation is no more, but General Electric is recognized for its consistent investments in developing leadership talent. At both organizations, if you were put into a management or leadership role, you received the appropriate training and development to prepare you to be effective not just in getting results for the business but in taking advantage of the human talent you lead to advance the goals of the business and allow the employees to develop as well. This was considered a wise investment for both the business and the human talent.

Although this may seem like ancient history, in the mid-1980s a shift saw training and development as a cost to be minimized and not an investment in the future of the business or that human talent. Over the years organizations have seen the folly of that perspective and have thrown money at the problem when times were flush, only to cut back again when times got tough. So there have been almost two generations of people who have not seen a consistent focus or investment in companies developing their talent. It's kept me in business for the last 20 years!

In my work as an executive leadership coach and in my previous corporate work, I did everything I could to research and explore what was being written about leadership and management and to stay as current as possible with new trends. Given the fact that I'm a bit of a "pack rat"—but a very organized one—I have accumulated a lot of information and concepts about the various elements of management and leadership. This has served my clients well, as I've been able to dip into this treasure trove of insights to provide the right material at the right time.

In an effort to maintain connections with the hundreds of people I have either served as a coach, worked with or just gotten to know over the last 30-plus years, I decided to create a blog about leadership on my website, www.executivecoachingconcepts.com, called the Coach's Corner. I always fancied myself a good wordsmith and a reasonably good writer; after all I was an English major for my first two years of college. But I really didn't know if what I was writing was hitting the mark and appreciated by the many folks I sent it to. As time went on, I got more and more positive feedback about how people valued what they read and often looked forward to my ideas and perspectives on the topics I chose.

From this work, a plan to create a book evolved. My purpose is to create a handy guide for managers and leaders that will provide specific insights on a wide range of topics. Each of the chapters is fairly short and each ends with some critical questions for you to ponder. I tend to think in models and I share them with my clients so they can become their own best coach. I have amassed a lot of information that I hope provides insights about ways to analyze and solve the many people challenges that come your way.

First, a brief note about the focus of this book. The following figure represents my view of what organizations are all about:

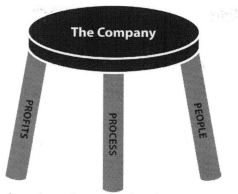

There are three key elements, the three Ps, in any company. They are:

- Process: This is all about the work or products that an organization creates. What you make and how you make it and all the various tools, techniques and manufacturing or creative methods are included here. A focus on continuous improvement is critical to ensure that you can produce what your clients are interested in better and faster.

- Profits: This has to do with all the accounting and financial wizardry that goes into ensuring the economic viability of any enterprise. Hopefully, the result is profits. Understanding and managing costs has to be the responsibility of everyone in your organization, and as a leader you need to ensure that the "economic literacy" of your workforce reflects a solid understanding of how your company does business and makes money.

- People: A leader I know often says, "We do everything we can to hire the best possible employees, but human beings keep showing up instead." This is a wonderful way of saying that as leaders we must navigate our way through all the people-related issues that are inherent in any company. As a matter of fact, when things blow up regarding profits and process, it is often the result of human error, that people thing. You might say this is a better representation of what can happen in organizations:

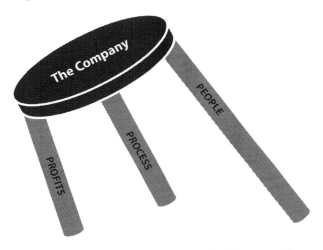

Now the stool is unbalanced. But I intended that. People issues can upset the whole team or company. So the focus of this book is the people things. I've always made sure not to attempt to give advice on areas that I don't have deep expertise in, so I leave the process and profits consulting to others.

Peter Drucker was one of the most profound and prolific writers about leadership over the last 100 years. The following quotation of his is on the back of my business card: "Management is doing things right. Leadership is doing the right things."

The distinction between leadership and management is very important, and the title of this book, *Discover the Joy of Leadership: A Practical Guide to Resolving Your Management Challenges*, reflects that. To me, leadership is exciting and daunting at the same time. A leader must look backward and learn from experience about what to do and not to do. A leader must also focus everyone on the present and ensure that the team or organization is carefully aligned around the goals or plans for their business. They must also look ahead and ideate, think incrementally or think big, assess risk, decide and plan. The demand to focus on past, present and future simultaneously is a very tall order! But that's how leaders can succeed and make their mark on an organization or even an industry.

The challenge is "doing things." The day-to-day work of managing, if not executed well, can crowd out the time and focus needed to be an effective leader. That is why, in addition to leadership, this book focuses on the following four management topics:

1. Making the best use of your **time**. In these days of infinite availability, where we are choked by the flow of texts and emails 24/7, it's easy to let time get away. Specific ideas and tools in these chapters will help you make better choices about the use of your time. If you can't get time under control, it's difficult to do any other management tasks well.

2. **Communicating** effectively on a consistent basis. The various elements of what I refer to as the "communication vibration" between the sender of a message and the person receiving it tend to get lost in this era of communicating primarily by email and texts or in poorly run meetings that waste time. The chapters about communication will help you understand how you can enhance the effectiveness of your messages.

3. Building better **relationships**. It's difficult to exert much influence over people we don't know well. When you haven't invested the time to get to know the people that matter within your organization and key thought leaders outside, you not only don't have a chance to develop trust with them but never learn much from them either. The readings in the relationship section will expand your thinking about the importance of relationship building and how to approach it.

4. Leading others through the inevitability of **change**. I don't know if this is the most disruptive era in the history of the world, but it often feels like that to me. Organizations change and morph almost continuously, and helping your team work through those changes is critical. You can't predict what will happen but you can get a good feel for how people react to change emotionally and psychologically. The chapters in this section will help you in that regard.

My pitch to my clients over the years has been that if I can help you improve your skills and knowledge on these management topics, you will be better prepared to lead. I hope you will find the section on leadership topics insightful and that the materials in this book will benefit you, your team and your organization and help you rediscover the Joy of Leadership. If you get stuck along the way, don't worry about it. I know a really good coach you can call.

LEADERSHIP

INTRO: Thoughts on Being a Leader

I HAVE BEEN VERY FORTUNATE in my careers to have met and worked with some excellent leaders and I learned something different from each one. They all exhibited great focus, intentionality and drive in all that they did and they were all able to channel the energy and momentum they marshalled to move organizations toward a common goal. Warren Bennis, a professor at the University of Southern California who has written extensively about leadership, said it best: "Leadership is the capacity to translate vision into reality." I have had opportunities to lead most of my life, from class president, business owner, chairman of my church congregation, the nation chief for Indian Princesses (I even had a headdress!) as well as various corporate leadership roles over the years. I'm a doer and a thinker and developed a reputation as somebody who made stuff happen. I admit I was not always the type of leader I wanted to be, but I developed my skills and style over the years and I helped many other people grow as leaders. It's been a very rewarding career in that regard and here are my collected thoughts on being a leader for people beginning their management careers and those who are already in leadership positions:

1. You will never know where your time goes until you are disciplined about tracking it and making decisions based on the fact of where it actually goes, not just your assumptions. What gets measured gets managed!

2. Be selfish about how you use your time so it is good for you, your team and your organization—in that order. Be appropriately selfish and be fully present when you are

3

with someone.

3. Talk about goals and performance metrics constantly in an aspirational manner. Keep people motivated and aligned by setting the right tone. Keep everyone's "eyes on the prize."

4. Take time to give feedback as soon as practical, shaping performance as you go. Don't wait for the annual performance appraisal. Recognize improvement and offer constructive suggestions as needed. Plan what you are going to say and listen to how others respond.

5. Be brave and ask for feedback. Accept feedback graciously and choose something you want to focus on to improve. Share your goals and solicit feedback along the way to shape your behavior. Seek candid lessons learned from all key projects or initiatives so you can do things better next time.

6. Stop doing something all the time. Consistently reevaluate what everyone is doing so that you can unclutter your work life. Do this regularly, at least once a quarter. Aim to eliminate enough things to save a modest two hours per week.

7. Take time to network within your organization and outside with thought leaders and key practitioners. This keeps people aware of what you're doing and also enhances your value to the organization based on the insights that you bring in.

8. Take the time to build relationships. Find out what's going on in other people's worlds and offer any assistance you can. Focus on how you can possibly assist them first. Learn to solicit input and ideas and ensure you're seeking the best solution and not just defending yours.

9. Learn how the change process works, anticipate the concerns of your staff and be prepared to communicate consistently.

Make change a learning experience and keep the dialogue going throughout. Consider:

- What exactly is going to change and how to state that unambiguously?
- What will really be different and who will be affected by what?
- Who might perceive the change as a loss of some sort? Losses hurt.

10. Build trust by being reliable and dependable, offering candid and constructive feedback when asked for it and maintaining confidential information when it is shared with you.

Many people have the idea that a leader sits at the top of the corporate or organizational pyramid. From here they issue orders, directions, suggestions and ideas that flow down throughout the rest of the pyramid. Their subordinates implement those ideas, as well as their own, and action moves on down the line to the lowest level supervisor. But I think that model needs to be stood on its head. What I am talking about is the concept of a servant leader, where leaders are at the bottom of the inverted pyramid and their job, in addition to setting direction, is to ensure that each layer above them in this inverted pyramid gets what it needs to ultimately serve the client or customer. I shared this in a meeting I was facilitating for the owner of a business, and the next day he came back to me and said that idea completely changed his view of his role. He said in many regards it was actually liberating for him to focus his energies on being of service to his team, allowing them to serve their customer better.

I do not have a specific model that I can share with you or my clients about the very best way to be a leader. I don't think that one exists. There are so many leadership books that come out every year from folks who have achieved remarkable individual feats, led major corporate successes or simply shared the stories of how they and their teams rose to the occasion to accomplish heroic or groundbreaking performances. Many of these can be inspiring, but you may never find yourself in a similar crucible of dynamic opportunity to achieve similar outcomes. However, there are still many elements of what leadership is all about that are common to any enterprise, regardless of its significance or potential impact. I think the following Celtic blessing is the finest aspirational description of what a leader should be:

For A Leader
May you have the grace and wisdom
To act kindly, learning
To distinguish between what is
Personal and what is not.
May you be hospitable to criticism.
May you never put yourself at the center of things.
May you act not from arrogance but out of service.
May you work on yourself,
Building up and refining the ways of your mind.
May those who work for you know
You see and respect them.
May you learn to cultivate the art of presence
In order to engage with those who meet you.
When someone fails or disappoints you,
May the graciousness with which you engage
Be their stairway to renewal and refinement.
May you treasure the gifts of the mind
Through reading and creative thinking
So that you continue as a servant of the frontier
Where the new will draw its enrichment from the old,
And you never become a functionary.
May you know the wisdom of deep listening,
The healing of wholesome words,

The encouragement of the appreciative gaze,
The decorum of held dignity,
The springtime edge of the bleak question.
May you have a mind that loves frontiers
So that you can evoke the bright fields
That lie beyond the view of the regular eye.
May you have good friends
To mirror your blind spots.
May leadership be for you
A true adventure of growth.

(From John O'Donohue. *To Bless This Space Between Us*.
New York, NY: Doubleday, 2008, pp. 151-153.)

I encourage you to read this poem several times and reflect on the depth of its messages and the challenges it provides for us all. This book's various selections on leadership will provide you a lot of ideas and insights that you can use to shape your own personal view and model of what works. Nothing that I have written will even come close to the eloquence of O'Donohue's blessing. Set a goal for yourself to be the best leader you can be. Be clear on the fact that the servant leader only knows about their effectiveness based on the feedback they get from those they serve.

If your actions inspire others to dream more, learn more, do more and become more, you are a leader.

—*John Quincy Adams*

What Is Your "Why?" How Purpose Should Shape Your Actions

Being busy does not always mean real work. The object of all work is production or accomplishment and to either of these ends, there must be forethought, system, planning, intelligence and honest purpose as well as perspiration. Seeming to do is not doing.
—Thomas A. Edison

Apple asked suppliers of the iPhone 6 and 6Plus to produce 80 million units by the end of 2014. Pre-orders for China accounted for 20 million.

How can Apple continue to succeed like this? By designing elegant products that are feature-laden and easy to use. What does Apple do so well? It creates and manufactures great computers and phones. But why is the world lining up for Apple products? Because it has consistently challenged the status quo and dared to think differently about what it produces for its customers. And this sense of purpose is critical to how we all should look at our work.

I was recently referred to a TED Talk by Simon Sinek called "Start with Why."[1] He laid out the case for what leaders should be focused on and asked the questions about Apple mentioned above. The bull's-eye of Sinek's model is WHY, and WHY is the key leadership focus for everything leaders should do.

Sinek made a distinction that resonated with me. He said leaders often have organizational power and authority and rely on those levers of power to drive the HOW and WHAT that get accomplished. But those who lead inspire us to follow them because we buy into the WHY they share with us. We want to follow them because of what WHY means for us, not them.

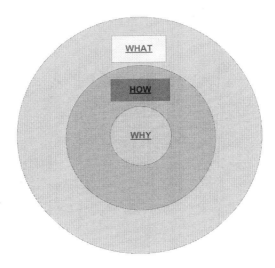

Sinek also stated that Martin Luther King, Jr., did not say he had a plan; but that he had a dream; and that is what people wanted to follow. They may have admired his speeches or his nonviolent approach, but his followers also wanted to live the dream, live in a country where everyone is treated fairly, regardless of the color of their skin. He challenged the status quo to create a new WHY.

But leading change requires that you reinforce the WHY and what's in it for everyone. The third part of Ken Follett's Century Trilogy, *The Edge of Eternity*,[2] covers the southern Freedom Riders, the followers of Dr. King, in 1961–62. The book is historical fiction but it shows how leaders must consistently reinforce the WHY and be relentless about it. The Freedom Riders were brave and determined people, but most important, they understood the reasons behind the causes they believed in.

Sinek's TED Talk made me think about my leadership experiences and the challenges I see with many of my clients. I led several key organizational changes in my career and in the two companies I have owned. I often spent time focused on the HOW and the WHAT and failed to leverage the WHY to gain support and build on the WHY as we progressed. The WHY is the purpose, cause or belief that creates the impetus for doing something. It can't be just to make more money or gain market share. Our purpose has to challenge us beyond that.

Instead of focusing on WHY, I relied on my organizational power and authority to sell changes and make the implementation as smooth and flawless as possible. I was probably afraid of objections that might crop up about the initiative after we began implementation and avoided having to defend the WHY for the changes I was leading.

A company I work with was conducting a leadership review of its portfolio companies. The purpose for these investments is to add talent, systems, expertise and support to help the companies realize their promise in their markets. Ultimately they will be sold to other firms that can build on their success. Each company has a well thought-out path to value (PTV) to help it focus on exploiting its promise. There was a scramble to get the current PTV for each company accurately stated for the review. Now, things change all the time in the marketplace, but the PTV affects each company's WHY and HOW. It struck me that a lack of clarity can be an issue for everyone involved in grooming these companies for success.

I realize that often work may not seem significant enough to warrant a reinforcement of its WHY. But I also believe leaders can lead effectively only when they align their teams to a path to value, a purpose or just a learning experience they can rally around.

Ask yourself:

- What is my WHY? What is my purpose or cause for doing what I do?

- Have I reinforced this to my team and updated my own path to value?

- Do I hide behind my HOW and WHAT instead of reinforcing my WHY?

Six Key Behavioral Observations about Leadership from Peter Drucker

Management is about arranging and telling.
Leadership is about nurturing and enhancing.
—Tom Peters

I am constantly trying to understand the changing nature of the demands on leaders and to see how the definition of effective leadership is evolving. But sometimes, it all goes back to the basics. Some of the best thought leaders have added to our collective understanding.

Peter Drucker (1909–2005) was a management consultant, educator and prolific author whose writings contributed to the philosophical and practical foundations of the modern corporation. He has been described as the founder of modern management and has had a profound influence on management education and leadership development worldwide. In the forward to *The Leader of the Future,*[3] Drucker said, "Regardless of their almost limitless diversity with respect to personality, style, abilities and interests, the effective leaders I have met, worked with and observed also *behaved* much the same way." Here are quotes about six key attributes of leaders Drucker described, along with my reflections and analysis:

1. "They did not start out with the question, 'What do I want?' They started out asking, 'What needs to be done?'"

Senior leaders have power and authority and many seek to make their mark on organizational performance. But true servant leaders provide strategy and direction and then concentrate on providing all the resources their teams need to fulfill the mission. It should never be about the ego of the leader.

13

2. "Then they asked, 'What can and should I do to make a difference?' This has to be something that both needs to be done and fits the leader's strengths and the way she or he is most effective."

Effective leaders have the self-knowledge to understand what they do really well and seek to exploit that ability for completing the goals. They know their individual team members well enough to help each of them do the same.

3. "They constantly asked, 'What are the organization's mission and goals? What constitutes performance and results in this organization?'"

Clarity about the results sought and how to measure good performance are topics that continually get reinforced through effective dialogue and interaction. Conflicts may always arise about options in pursuing the outcomes, but great leaders relish these discussions as a way to teach and to help the leadership skills of everyone involved blossom along the way.

4. "They were extremely tolerant of diversity in people and did not look for carbon copies of themselves. It rarely even occurred to them to ask, 'Do I like or dislike this person?' But they were totally—fiendishly—intolerant when it came to a person's performance, standards and values."

I have seen people's careers derail because they could not perform, and everyone understands how that can happen. But I have also witnessed good performers get derailed when they cut corners, mistreat others or act like asses. Some organizations put less emphasis on standards and values than performance, and that always shows up in the quality of the culture. The best leaders I know are fiendish protectors of their companies' culture, regardless of performance.

5. "They were not afraid of strength in their associates. They gloried in it. Whether they had heard of it or not, their motto was what Andrew Carnegie wanted to have put on his tombstone: 'Here lies a man who attracted better people into his service than he was himself.'"

Leaders must have followers or they are not really leaders. The leader and his followers are a team. Business leaders should be similar to coaches of great athletic teams. The best leaders mold and mentor others into becoming better leaders.

6. "One way or another, they submitted themselves to the 'mirror test'—that is, they made sure that the person they saw in the mirror in the morning was the kind of person they wanted to be, respect and believe in. This way they fortified themselves against the leader's greatest temptations—to do things that are popular rather than right and to do petty, mean, sleazy things."

There is nothing easy about being a leader, and we each must hope our inner rudder is steered in the appropriate direction. One key thing that every successful captain has is a strong lieutenant that she or he knows will provide the right kind of advice and honest feedback. The courage to do the tough things makes the triumphs all the sweeter! Popularity is not leadership—great results are.

Ask yourself:

- Are you and the team clear about what constitutes great performance and results?

- How tolerant are you of a good performer who does not manage according to the values you have set?

- What one thing can you do that would make looking in the mirror more satisfying for you?

Six Things Tightrope Walkers and Leaders Should Have in Common

High expectations are the key to everything.

—Sam Walton

ONE EARLY NOVEMBER NIGHT in 2014, Nik Wallenda walked a tightrope for two city blocks across the Chicago River between two high-rises at a height of 600 feet. A friend of mine and I watched in a crowd of about 65,000, and it was carried live on the Discovery Channel. The feat took six minutes and 51 seconds to accomplish. His next trick was to walk blindfolded between two towers at 500 feet, which he did in one minute, 17 seconds.

Wallenda's walk made me think of what leaders have to face all the time. He is from a famous family of daredevils who have seen their share of tragedy. I'm sure some leaders feel like they are walking on tightropes in their adventures in leading, although their struggles will never be a matter of life and death 600 feet above a river.

As I watched Wallenda, I marveled at the network of guy wires that held the main rope in place. These stretched for more than a block in either direction and then up 600 feet. To me, the main rope represented the leader and the guy wires were the subordinates to a leader and supportive of his or her vision or plan. The reality is that Wallenda never could have executed his amazing feat without the incredible efforts of so many to make it happen.

What does Wallenda's team get for his feats? I have no idea what it is like to work for a daredevil or how they are rewarded. But I do know leaders are not leaders if they have no followers, so I considered what a leader's team needs to know to create a truly effective executive group. Larry Bossidy had a 30-year career at General Electric and

17

then became the CEO of Allied Signal. He wrote an insightful article in the *Harvard Business Review*, "What Your Leader Expects of You—And What You Should Expect in Return."[4] Here's what he said, followed by some observations of mine:

What My Direct Reports Can Expect from Me

Provide clarity of direction. "If I'm the leader, it's my job to communicate clearly where the business is going, why, and what the benefits will be if we accomplish what we set out to achieve."

There is an old Native American saying, "If you don't know where you are going, any path will do." Clarity and a commitment to reaffirming and adjusting the path along the way are critical.

Set goals and objectives. "An executive may assume he's doing a good job, but he can't know for sure that his boss would agree if he has no specific goals and objectives to strive for."

Alignment of focus and efforts is critical. Within the boundaries that are set for any objective, there is lots of room for creativity and accomplishment. Without alignment, you get chaos.

Give frequent, specific and immediate feedback. "When I give feedback, I'm signaling to people that I'm interested in their growth and that I see a path for their future. Employees shouldn't have to wait for an annual review to learn how they are doing, and if the feedback is going to help drive their growth, then it needs to be as specific as possible."

Leaders need to have the metrics and the feedback loops to measure effectiveness and progress. Leaders should seek feedback from their team as well. There must be an atmosphere of openness and trust to support such candid dialogue.

Be decisive and timely. "Decisiveness isn't useful if it isn't timely. People should expect me to make decisions as soon as I have the information I need, and not be careless or impetuous but to give clear, unambiguous answers."

Be sure you have agreement from the folks that matter so you can say, "At this time, with this information, we have all we need to make this decision." But be sure you know when to say, "Why hurry?" if you are not sure. Business is not about eliminating risk; it's about managing it.

Be accessible. "If I expect people to keep me informed about what's going on, then I need to be available when they need me. It's certainly in my interest."

The most effective leaders are always busy, but they do not let their calendars control their work or personal lives. One of the most successful CEOs I have ever met will respond to me in 24 hours or sooner if he's not traveling internationally.

Demonstrate honesty and candor. "People spend far too much time figuring out how to tell others something unpleasant, how to deliver the news in a diplomatic way. If I can say something sensitively and diplomatically, so much the better. But if I can't, I owe it to my employee to say it anyway."

To be candid, you must have trust. One key element of a trusting relationship is that others can count on you to provide candid, constructive feedback when asked, when a teachable moment presents itself or when the situation demands it. Honesty must be an expectation of all on the team.

Ask yourself:

- What kind of tightrope team are we? Does everyone on my team know what success looks like?

- As a leader, how would my team rate me on these six expectations?

- What is the one thing I can do to be a more effective leader based on Bossidy's expectations of a leader?

Three Survival Lessons from a Vietnam Prisoner of War

You will never do anything in this world without courage.
It is the greatest quality of the mind next to honor.
—Aristotle

For many years, I've worked with a prominent financial advisory team that manages more than $7 billion for its clients. Jerry, a member of the team, announced his retirement and gave a presentation at the company's annual meeting. He shared his experiences as a prisoner of war in Vietnam for 5½ years. Jerry is a bright, friendly and positive fellow, and he and I have talked about the connection he developed with Senator John McCain, a fellow prisoner. I've never felt comfortable about delving too deeply into his experiences, but Jerry's presentation, which he gives to various groups, was enlightening and instructive for everyone. I'd like to share his story with you because it reflects on some key leadership attributes we all should consistently consider.

Shortly after Jerry's arrival in one of the several prisons where he endured years of abuse, deprivation and hardship, another prisoner impressed on him that the last thing he ought to do was feel sorry for himself. All the other men in the prison were in the same situation but, more important, feeling sorry for himself would result in only one thing—his death. We have all had difficult challenges in business and life, but few of us encounter situations that rise to the level of life and death!

The other prisoner said to Jerry, "There are three key things that you have to have to survive: faith, commitment and pride." He said that you cannot choose what happens to you but you can always choose how you will react. Jerry tells his remarkable story of resilience, camaraderie and the dangerous games of resistance prisoners played with the often sadistic guards they encountered. Here's how these three things are also critical to your success, regardless of the setbacks or challenges you may be facing.

Faith

Faith is not about being religious, necessarily, but you've got to believe in what you are doing. Open your mind to inspiration or serendipity, whether it's divinely inspired or not, since solutions can come from anywhere. There's no such thing as a congregation of one person. So reach out and share with others on your journey. Jerry's stories of how prisoners banded together to communicate in clever, subtle but effective ways are great examples of how common beliefs and needs can drive success and survival.

Commitment

Most people will never have to commit themselves to survival in brutal conditions like a POW must endure. But whatever goal, project or level of customer satisfaction you demand for your clients or personal and professional growth that you aspire to, you have to be really all in to make it happen. It is rare that half-hearted efforts result in exceptional performance.

Pride

Being too proud is one of the seven deadly sins, but you have to demand the best of yourself in all that you do. Pride in yourself is not as beneficial as taking pride in what you do. As a leader, you are always judged by what you say and do. Always give your best, but remember that the biggest barrier to progress is perfection. Get the best out of your team by figuring out what they can learn or the how they can grow from experiences, just like you have done yourself.

One of the key things that really resonated with me about Jerry's stories was his commitment to himself, his fellow prisoners and our country. Jerry's experiences are inspiring to me, and they certainly reinforce a key perspective that I share with all my clients as they decide on the goals to focus on. In the goal-setting process, I ask my clients how the pursuit of any goal will benefit them, their team and their organization. And I always stress that they focus on the potential benefits in that order. That may sound self-serving, but that is the reality of how we assess any situation. Jerry was very focused on his own survival, but his care for his fellow prisoners and representing his country were always clearly in his line of sight. As you focus your energy on your work, I encourage you to do your own analysis of the potential impact of achieving any goal for yourself as well.

Ask yourself:

- Do I believe in what I'm doing? Am I confident that the energy and efforts of our team will have the intended positive benefits, regardless of the project we are engaged in?

- Have I allocated the right amount of resources, time, and focus to demonstrate my commitment to making things happen well?

- Upon completion of any significant task or effort, will I be able to say that I am proud of what we have accomplished?

MANAGE LIKE A FOUR-EYED FISH
FOUR QUESTIONS TO HELP YOU LOOK ABOVE AND BELOW THE SURFACE OF THINGS

Leadership is the capacity to translate vision into reality.
—WARREN BENNIS

I RECENTLY HEARD ABOUT the existence of a four-eyed fish named the anableps. Its natural habitat stretches from southern Mexico to Honduras to northern South America. It has two eyes that are raised above the top of its head and are divided into two different parts so it can see above and below the water surface at the same time. See, you learn something every day!

But what in the world could the existence of a four-eyed fish have to do with improving your ability to manage? Well, when you think about the world of management, especially in today's crazed work environment where the volume of tasks and the expectations of getting it all done immediately can make it difficult to keep up, we could all use two sets of eyes (and perhaps two sets of ears and hands). If you manage the work of others, you have a trifecta of challenges on your hands—performance, process and people.

• **Performance:** You're responsible for the outcomes of the work that you and your team are performing. There are issues of quality, quantity, timeliness and usually revenues and a budget. Significant effort is required to keep up with all the variables that affect these measures and how they are accounted for.

• **Process:** You and your team work with processes all the time. Some of these, like financial and other reporting mechanisms, are determined by the organization. Some are more under your control or influence as a part of how you and your team do what you have to do. It takes great focus to understand how your processes can result in increased productivity and performance. Given the complexities of many operating systems and the fact that new features and improvements are constantly being made, getting more from your processes is a significant challenge as well.

• **People:** A client of mine likes to say that you hire employees, but human beings always seem to show up instead. Many managers have spans of control that are too broad to keep tabs on the accomplishments and needs of all their staff, especially when the challenges of staying on top of performance and process are added to the mix.

Today one of the key workplace issues is the level of disengagement that many employees feel. Much disengagement can be traced to the fact that managers are so challenged with performance and process that dealing with people gets short shrift. People are "under-led" because managers don't know how to manage people that well or because performance and processes are allowed to consume all their time. It's not unusual to find managers who are really good at handling things, but not adept at handling people.

The anableps can see above the water and below the water at the same time. This adaptation allows it to eat insects that are readily available on the surface of the water as well as diatoms and other small fishes below the surface. These foot-long freshwater fish flourish by being able to take advantage of both sources of nutrition.

Most managers do well at looking below the surface at performance and process. But I challenge managers to use the other part of their vision to look above the surface and focus more effectively on the people they are trying to manage. To do this, managers will have to allocate at least some time each week to thinking about each person who reports to them or, better yet, chatting with them about their work. You know how much you hate it when you have to write reviews of everyone's performance over a few days, once a year? Space out such evaluations and make them a regular part of your work week. Here are four key questions to consider asking each employee who reports to you:

1. What part of your duties do you like the most and why?
2. What part of your duties do you have the most trouble with and why?
3. What is the one thing I could do to help you learn and grow?
4. If I were able to provide learning and growth, how would it help you, the team and the company?

When you actively engage employees about these four questions, you can be sure they'll expect you to respond to their issues or concerns. Handling these expected responses can get difficult, causing some managers to avoid dialogue with their staff. You may think you don't have much power to change anything to assist an individual employee, but here are a couple of suggestions to get you started:

• Just ask your staff the first two questions above about duties they like and those they struggle with. Plan to do this for each member of your team and use the feedback to rebalance workloads so people get to do more of the things they like and are good at. If you find any common themes about the more challenging parts of the duties, you can investigate training or one-on-one support for those who need help. You may even be able to ask the member or members of the team that are the most skilled in these areas to provide the training. That can look good for their annual review and perhaps their resume.

• Question number three is something that each employee should be asked at least once a year. Again, if you find common needs among the team, everybody wins. But remember that access to information, exposure to other parts of the organization or leading a small effort can be opportunities that provide experiences but cost little. Just be sure that you follow up on everything you say you will do to help your staff learn and grow.

• Question number four is critical in helping employees understand the interrelationships between what's good for them, the team and the organization. They may not care about the impact beyond themselves, but you need to help reinforce the connections and enhance their understanding.

So elevate your line of sight, look above the water, above the insanity or the general everyday hubbub that is your work world. Be sure that the people who work for you are the focus of these efforts.

Ask yourself:

• Do I know what each person on my team really likes about their work?

• Do I know where they struggle?

• What can I do to help?

THE PERILS OF PERFECTIONISM
AND SIX THINGS TO DO ABOUT IT

A leader is best when people barely know he exists, when his work is done, his aim fulfilled, they will say: we did it ourselves.
—LAO TZU, ANCIENT CHINESE PHILOSOPHER

A JULY 24, 2014, POST BY Michael Hyatt on his website, Intentional Leadership, entitled "The Paradigm Shift That Helped Me Defeat Perfectionism Once and for All" really caught my attention. I have studied the effects of perfectionism on leadership for many years and Hyatt's description of his experience was insightful. In my experience, people with perfectionistic tendencies tend to be very detail-oriented, very reliable and real workhorses who can really produce. But their uncommonly high expectations for themselves make it hard for those around them, much less their subordinates, to live up to their standards. This sows seeds of discord and disappointment for the perfectionist and those they interact with. It is a personality trait that needs to be identified and managed, or it is certain to become a career limiter for those who have it.

Hyatt moved from a career in publishing to becoming a thought leader about leadership. He realized that the very deliberate process of bringing a book to market requires the coordination of editors, proofers, designers, printers, marketers, publicists and salespeople.

When you consider creating 10,000 or 1 million copies of a book, all that due diligence makes sense. In the world of internet marketing and thought leadership, however, a very deliberate approach can be too time-consuming.

When he spoke of the paradigm shift, he was talking about how to shift his production methods to fit the internet world. Here are the three things he suggested that can help you "break free from the perfection trap":

1. **Change your perspective.** Reframe your approach to projects, and remember you can adapt and update things as needed online.
2. **Narrow your focus.** Don't try to do too much. Do fewer things well and avoid burnout.
3. **Don't confuse perfection with excellence.** Maintain high standards but don't seek the unattainable goal of perfection.

Several years ago I was asked to coach a group of high-level technical influencers in an organization. One of the assessments I used showed that each of the three men had the exact same profile out of the more than 20 possible profiles. That's more than a coincidence. It turns out that each person demonstrated a high degree of focus on getting tasks done and had a significant focus on process as well. There is a natural tension between those two areas of focus, and this conflict fits the more common psychological profile of perfectionism.

I did some research and found an excellent book, *Too Perfect: When Being In Control Gets Out of Control,*[5] by Mallinger and DeWyze. I began to see more and more perfectionists in the leaders I served.

The perfectionist has high needs for control that emanate from fears:

Fear of Being Found Out[6]

Perfectionists think, "Maybe I'm not the expert and don't have all the answers. Perhaps others who get to really know me will find out."

- Like in *The Wizard of Oz*: "Ignore that man behind the curtain!"
- Fear of errors or making a wrong decision or move
- A need to know and follow the rules
- A need for order or firmly established routines
- An inclination to worry, rumination and doubt

Fear of Trusting

To protect themselves against the vulnerability of trusting, perfectionists are wary, doubting others' motives, honesty and reliability.

- Emotional guardedness
- A need to be above criticism—moral, professional, or personal

Fear of Dependency

Perfectionists think if they are dependent, they sacrifice some autonomy, some loss of control over their lives.

- A heightened awareness of being pressured or controlled by others
- Cautiousness

If these descriptors resonate with you either about yourself or someone you lead, do not despair. Many perfectionistic tendencies have beneficial outcomes in the business world. But a strength carried to an extreme can be a vice.

The ultimate irony—and tragedy—of perfectionism is that it simply doesn't work. It's supposed to earn you rave reviews and exempt you from criticism. Instead, it damages your work and your relationships and puts you under unrelenting pressure. Perfectionists often are anxious about their encounters with others, giving them the impression of being cool and aloof and sometimes conceited.

Six Suggestions for Perfectionists

If you've concluded that your perfectionism is hurting you, you can make changes.

Here are six things to help you avoid the perils of perfectionism:

1. Remind yourself that no one and nothing can be 100 percent dependable.

2. Aim for average. Under-promise and over-deliver (but not too much).

3. Don't get tripped up by your tendency to think in terms of extremes. Instead of either/or as a way to analyze everything, find the middle.

4. Try to be conscious that your guarded behavior is likely to cause the very rejection, isolation and unloved feelings you fear.

5. It takes determination and patience to become less guarded. Avoid worry, rumination and doubt.

6. Use "Thought Stopping."[7] When you recognize negative thoughts, think of how it makes you feel—painful, anxious, angry or uncomfortable, not relieved or satisfied—distracting you from more positive, constructive thoughts. Pull on a rubber band on your wrist and say "Stop" aloud. Inhale deeply, and relax. Wait 15 seconds and repeat, "Worrying won't help." Do this until you move to something more productive.

Ask yourself:

- Which fears of a perfectionist may I be harboring?

- How can I change my habits to control my tendency for perfectionism?

- Am I willing to ask a friend or colleague to "catch me in the act" and help me overcome the negative aspects of perfectionism?

THE NO ASSHOLE RULE

In the course of my observation, the disputing, contradicting
and confuting people are generally unfortunate in their affairs.
They get victory sometimes, but they never get good will,
which would be of more use to them.
—BENJAMIN FRANKLIN

I AM PROUD OF MY ASSOCIATION with Paul Purcell, chairman of Robert
W. Baird & Co., a financial services firm headquartered in Milwaukee, Wisconsin. I met Purcell shortly after he was named president
of Baird, more than 17 years ago. Baird has grown and prospered remarkably well under his leadership, and total revenues now top $1 bil-
lion. More important, Baird has been recognized by *Fortune* magazine
as one of the "Top 100 Places to Work" for the last 13 years.

One thing Purcell has consistently spoken about—a key part of his
leadership philosophy—is his "no asshole rule" (NAHR). Purcell was
an investment banker for 22 years before he came to Robert W. Baird.
The first 18 were great years. That firm prospered and he developed
many lasting relationships during his tenure there. Purcell is keen on
developing solid, trusting relationships and nurturing them over time.

The last four years at his previous firm were challenging as the
market turned down. Many senior bankers left, and some replacements
did not fit the culture that Purcell valued so much. In addition, the
firm paid premiums to attract many of these people and was "robbing
Peter to pay Paul," a further affront to the culture. The difference in
the style of the newer members of the team was manifested in the
type of clients they did business with and was viewed by the veterans
as pulling client standards down. In addition, the newer bankers

spent 20 to 30 percent of their time justifying their pay. This wasted productivity and further chipped away at the culture.

From this experience, Purcell became a culture warrior and has nurtured and reinforced the Baird culture since he moved there. He crystallized his concern about a specific brand of cultural misfit in the "Baird Business Update," the company's internal newsletter in 2007, where he reflected on a previous interview with *Fortune* magazine: "My definition of an asshole (AH) is anybody who puts themselves in front of the client or in front of their partners at Baird. One of the best parts of our firm is that we don't tolerate people who are not team players."

Some people may object to Purcell's use of the word "asshole." Some may think senior executives should not use such crude language in regular discourse or, worse yet, in print because it may be considered rude or because it diminishes individuals and the institutions they represent. Purcell responds, "I apologize if the language offended anybody, but I was thrilled that *Fortune* printed it because I do think it says that we really stand for something as a firm." I assure you that Paul is a consummate gentleman and does not need to use coarse language for effect, but he's not backing off his focus on preventing the impact of AHs at Robert W. Baird.

Purcell says AHs are consistently full of themselves and arrogant. He has made it a company policy to avoid hiring AHs via a rigorous screening process and to ask people to leave if they develop into AHs later on. He has said that it is hard to ask someone to leave whose skills no longer measure up to the organizational challenges but who are good people. However, it is never hard for him to get rid of AHs.

In preparing for a meeting I was having with Purcell in 2010, I happened to see a book on Amazon called *The No Asshole Rule: Building a Civilized Workplace and Surviving One That Isn't,*[8] by Robert I. Sutton, Ph.D., a professor of management science and engineering at Stanford University. Intrigued, I bought a copy and gave it to Purcell when we met. He wasn't pleased because he claimed he was going to write just such a book when he retired! (By the way, in his next book, *Good*

Boss, Bad Boss: How to Be the Best and Learn from the Worst,[9] Sutton interviewed Purcell about his NAHR.)

So how do you determine who is an AH? The Supreme Court's definition of pornography is insightful here: We know it when we see it. The same thing is true of AHs. They have some common traits, such as using personal insults with some frequency, resorting to threats and intimidation, being excessively harsh in tone in email, intentionally humiliating others in public and showing indifference to others by treating them like they are invisible. Based on your own experiences, I am sure you can add to this list, but I think we all get it. In short, I would say they are bullies.

As a leader, you probably pride yourself on your resiliency in dealing with stressors at work. Any individual demonstration of the above behaviors is possibly tolerable, but a constantly repeating pattern is corrosive. "If you permit it, you promote it" is a phrase I heard recently. What's even worse is the unpredictability of the behavior of AHs. In the second chapter of *The No Asshole Rule*, Sutton looks at the costs of sustained AH behavior, which I summarize as:

- The harm caused to the victims of the AH directly;
- The effects on those who witness this behavior, especially in intimidating others, making them afraid to speak for fear of attack or retribution;
- Management's time spent counseling both the AH and the victims rather than engaging in productive work;
- The potential cost to the organization for allowing a "hostile work environment" to exist and the potential litigation costs;
- The very real impact of reducing the effective flow of information and ideas where AHs are allowed to flourish.

I am sure you can add to this list of corrosive behaviors and their consequences. When you add up all the potential costs and effects, you can see why the NAHR can be so valuable. But how practical is the NAHR?

Twice I have been asked by clients to be of service to some leaders in their organizations who had run into problems because of their behavior. I explained the concept of the NAHR and asked if it possibly applied to the employees we were discussing. (I've worked with some challenging clients and fired only one in 18 years, but I don't want to work with an AH any more than anyone else does. If the individual in question is really an AH and has badly burned bridges with an organization, engaging me might be throwing money away.) I suggested they review a test that Sutton developed to decide if someone they were dealing with was an AH.[10] This valuable quiz helps identify key behaviors that can assist you in helping potential AHs from derailing or in beginning the tough choice of separating an AH from the organization. My hope is that this can be an enlightening, but seldom used, diagnostic.

The reality is that we come into contact with AHs from time to time or have to tolerate them in our work world. Chapter 5 of Sutton's *No Asshole Rule* is "Tips for Surviving Nasty People and Workplaces."[11] I would encourage you to review the whole chapter, but here are a few key ideas:

• **Develop Indifference and Emotional Detachment.** If you are in a job where you feel exploited and demeaned, toughen your emotional veneer and get things done with as little personal involvement as possible.

• **Fight and Win the Right Small Battles.** De-escalate the situation by refusing to get sucked into any tension as it rises. Re-education involves reminding the AH of their inappropriate behavior and seeking support of management to deal with them.

• **Limit Your Exposure.** Spend as little time as possible with these jerks.

Lots of AHs have been richly rewarded, and sometimes justice never seems to come for them. But their comeuppance happens over time. Karma will even things out! It is everyone's job to ensure that AHs are confronted about their behavior and how inconsistent it is with the values and expectations of the organization (provided it is!).

As you reflect on this challenging topic, ask yourself:

- Am I honest enough to admit to some AH behavior of my own? Is this a rare flare-up or a more regular occurrence? Can I adjust?

- Am I willing to address the behaviors of AHs on my team despite the fact that they may perform well and contribute to the success of the organization?

- If I want a culture that embraces a no asshole rule, am I prepared to lead an effort to root out AH behavior and create a zero tolerance policy?

SUCCESS IS LEASED . . .

Success isn't owned; it's leased and you pay rent every day.
— J.J. WATT, ALL-PRO FOOTBALL PLAYER FOR THE HOUSTON TEXANS

I THINK WATT MEANS that you have to continue to earn the respect of others for your contributions and wisdom and that you can never rest on your laurels. He was referring to his dedication and all the hard work it took to make himself physically and mentally capable of staying at the very top of the violent and challenging world of the National Football League.

Similarly, business competition is global and instantaneous. The currency of your connections with your clients and team requires ongoing effort, and ours is a "what have you done for me lately?" world now more than ever. Several years ago, Ed Gubman wrote *The Engaging Leader: Winning with Today's Free Agent Workforce.*[12] Gubman uses multiple examples to suggest that the management of talent in the corporate world should more closely align itself with how professional sports teams manage their roster of talent. It's a challenging way of looking at a world for knowledge workers rather than athletes who, by definition, see their physical talents diminish over time, whereas knowledge workers are thought to gain wisdom, experience and pattern recognition to add value to their organizations. Taking a professional sports team approach would be such a shock to the system of our current world of work that I can't grasp all of the implications.

But within 10 years the millennials in our workforce will outnumber the baby boomers who, for the most part, are currently running most major organizations. This major population shift will be accompanied by a generational focus that is much less oriented towards respect or deference for those who may feel that they have "paid their dues." When I was in my early 20s there was a countercultural belief about not trusting anyone over 30. That had associated with it much more of a revolutionary zeal, but the lack of deference today is much more a reflection of the fact that the standards of excellence or organizational effectiveness keep changing so rapidly that it's hard to say what you can rely on.

Marshall Goldsmith's book *What Got You Here Won't Get You There*[13] identifies 20 habits that he describes as "transactional flaws performed by one person against another." I usually share the 20 habits with my clients as part of my initial work with them because I believe that Goldsmith has identified some common behaviors that simply get in the way of an individual's success. The last of these 20 is "an excessive need to be me: exulting our faults as virtues simply because they're who we are."

Often, highly skilled individuals who have developed business practices that have led to substantial success can be reluctant to adjust, much less conform, to new work processes because they cling to "my" way of doing things that had been so successful. They disregard the downline impact on the many people who support their efforts. Some of their subordinates have told me they have been forced into all-night vigils and wasted weekends just waiting for information from such leaders before they can complete their part of some tasks.

Is it hubris or selfishness on the part of those that continue to revel in the need to be "me"? I don't think so because I believe these smart and capable people truly believe that their past practices were integral to their current success. But the other aspect of this behavioral choice is that many of them feel they are entitled to "be me," that they have earned the right to do things their way. There is a growing and substantial resistance in today's workplace to anyone claiming they are entitled to a position, respect or deference in our society as a whole just for being who they are, even if they are the leaders in an organization.

I am a traditionalist by nature and have always believed that people should be able to earn the respect of others based on their past performance and credentials. But in this rapidly changing world, one of the fastest-changing elements is the obsolescence of experiences and former victories unless an individual can continue to succeed in the crucible of escalating expectations. Younger generations in the workforce are early adopters and adapters, and to them, resting on yesterday's accomplishments is as passé as using yesterday's technologies.

My mentor in my late 20s and early 30s shaped my career like no one else and invested in me professionally and personally. When I was first told I was going to work with him, my predominant emotion was fear. He scared me. That was eclipsed by respect as I got to work with him for several years and we developed a good friendship as well. He was a remarkable and fascinating fellow. But several years after he retired—and he always wanted to talk shop—I recognized that the suggestions he had were no longer current and only modestly relevant. He was never trying to tell me what to do, but as much as I admired him, his perspective just reinforced my desire to stay as current as I possibly could.

So my message centers around two conflicting trends. The first is the idea that we are entitled to be "me" because of past accomplishments. The second is that no one has a right to feel that they deserve or are owed any respect. I do not have any suggestions for how to deal with this growing conflict beyond basic civility and professionalism in every business situation.

Ask yourself:

- Do I feel that my contributions to my team and organization reflect the current values that are expressed in the marketplace?

- How much do I bank on my history of success for maintaining my current level of rewards? Do I feel entitled?

- Do I invest some time in trying to understand and connect with the younger generations that will be replacing me someday?

- If I am in those younger ranks, what's my attitude about the generations that have preceded me?

FIVE LEADERSHIP REGRETS I HOPE WE CAN ALL AVOID

Man is truly great when he acts from the passions.
—BENJAMIN DISRAELI (1804-1881)

I RECENTLY CAME ACROSS an interesting article, "The Top 5 Regrets of the Dying,"[14] which are listed below:

1. I wish I'd had the courage to live a life true to myself, not the life others expected of me.
2. I wish I hadn't worked so hard.
3. I wish I'd had the courage to express my feelings.
4. I wish I had stayed in touch with my friends.
5. I wish that I had let myself be happier.

My parents passed away a decade ago after a slow decline during the previous decade. My father was pretty stoic and never waxed philosophically about any regrets. My mother tragically lost her ability to communicate when I was 12, so there were none expressed there either. But during my career, and especially recently, I have seen a lot of clients and friends nearing the end of their working careers. I thought about what regrets seasoned leaders should consciously avoid now so the pangs of potential regret could be muted. Here are some thoughts for you to ponder now about how to leverage your influence to make your mark on the world that is good for you, your family and friends, your organization and your community.

Live the life you want.

When you are focused primarily on those things you have developed a passion for, great things happen. You become passionate about something because it captures your imagination and you develop an almost unconscious competence for it. It is in everyone's best interest to provide as much time and focus for that and to shed the parts of your work that can be best left to others. It's not just about jettisoning the tough or unpleasant parts of your job but about finding others for whom that work fulfills their passion or skills and may be critical to their development.

Find time to smell the roses now.

As they say, on your deathbed no man ever said he wished he could have spent more time at the office. Make some choices and provide time for your personal, professional and spiritual development. Take that class, make that trip and go watch your children's activities as they grow up. Don't be so afraid of what you'll miss at the office. Work to live; don't live to work.

Express yourself more effectively everywhere, including your feelings.

Be willing to assert yourself because you have something to say that matters—not just to be heard. Don't pick fights, but stand up for what you believe. I recently came across a very interesting way of thinking about this. In his upcoming book, Marshall Goldsmith asks this question to provide structure for what you may wish to weigh in on: Am I willing at this time to make the investment required to make a positive difference on this topic?[15]

Stay in touch with friends.

I came across a saying not long ago: "Whose door could you knock on that would not let you in?" Granted, we may have lost touch with some folks, but it does not mean we cannot reach out and make an effort to reconnect. Facebook and other tools can create great ways to find folks who would be flattered to be thought of. A true friend can be someone with whom the connection was forged long ago. Make it happen.

Happiness is a choice. Decide to be happy!

Do not confuse being content with being happy. Our fears and worries often constrain the range of choices we perceive ourselves to have. Your choice to be happy does not deny others their right to be happy, too. It's not a zero-sum game. Look for the joy in things. Laugh and have a little more fun.

I hope that by considering this now, everybody will shed a few regrets down the road.

Ask yourself:

- To what extent am I acting "from my passions" rather than just doing my job?

- Am I finding time to "smell the roses" now or am I waiting patiently for the time to be right?

- When was the last time I reached out to an old friend? What happened?

CAN "BIG DATA" HELP EMPLOYEE RETENTION?

Employees who believe that management is concerned about them
as a whole person—not just an employee—are more productive,
more satisfied, more fulfilled. Satisfied employees mean satisfied
customers, which leads to profitability.
—ANNE M. MULCAHY

YOU NEVER KNOW WHERE inspiration may come from. I saw this quote and thought it was a telling insight about the need for investing in developing employees in general and, given my interests, managers and leaders. The best corporations, like General Electric, my former employer, have consistently invested in developing their leadership talent. When times are flush for an organization, such expenditures are easier to justify. When times are tight, these expenses are viewed less like investments and more like costs to be controlled.

Our economy seems to be humming along very nicely. The unemployment rate continues to fall and the demand for talent is increasing. A recent article in *The Wall Street Journal*, "The Algorithm That Tells the Boss Who Might Quit,"[16] reflected on the costs of this reality:

- As the employment picture improves, companies are focusing more on retaining workers, largely because replacing them is costly. The median cost of turnover for most jobs is about 21 percent of an employee's annual salary, according to the Center for American Progress, a liberal-leaning think tank.

- William Wolf, Credit Suisse's global head of talent acquisition and development, says a one-point reduction in unwanted attrition rates saves the bank $75-$100 million per year.

This article explains how companies are using big data to try to understand organizational trends and, in this case, trying to create retention predictions to prevent employee flight risks. In other words, which work factors can help us understand who may be most at risk for leaving the organization and what can be done to retain good talent and reduce employee replacement costs? Although such sophisticated analysis might be expected to identify one or two clear causes for employee turnover, simple answers rarely emerge from the almost infinite variables of organization structure, tenure of employees, dynamics of the industry and technological change.

Rachel Silverman and Nikki Walker, the authors of this article, identified several interesting variables, but none can be generalized across a broader population in various companies. Rarely did any single piece of data prove to be substantially predictive. But here are a few points that did come up repeatedly:

- An employee's connection to the team

- The manager's performance and the size of the team an employee is on. (In one case, there was a spike in attrition on larger teams with lower-rated managers.)

- Employees who had waived benefit coverage

- Employees who felt that their jobs were not accurately described when they were hired

- Employees who had to relocate for a job

- Employees who went through significant job transitions, such as a promotion, or personal milestones, such as maternity leave

The article also quoted John Callery, director of people analytics at AOL Inc., which recently started working with workforce analytics firm Visier Inc., on a program to help predict attrition down to the individual employee. Callery said, "Our goal is to never say the only reason we are coming to talk to you is because an algorithm told us to do so."

So why don't managers have a better feel for retention risks? Several key variables limit the effectiveness of managers in dealing with this important leadership responsibility:

- Managers' span of control, or the number of people that managers are responsible for, is too large for them to have detailed insight about each employee.

- Many employees work remotely, even in other countries, and contact is primarily electronic or voice, not in person.

- Many managers must split their time between leading others' work and doing their own work. As levels have been flattened in many organizations and administrative support has been reduced by using technology, the time demands for most managers have increased dramatically.

- Improved networking skills and advanced technologies regarding job opportunities may create irresistible attractions for employees.

- For many managers, options for rewarding employees or increasing engagement may be limited. Cost controls in some organizations and managers' lack of creativity contribute to this problem. Managers need help to expand their range of options.

Retention of talent, especially as it becomes scarcer, must be an organizational imperative. In the depths of the downturn in 2008, the perspective was that every employee was replaceable so many organizations gave short shrift to the concept of employee retention. Not so now.

Ask yourself:

- Do I have a good feel for the relative job satisfaction for each member of my team?

- Do I have a good sense of how engaged each member of my team is?

- What options do I have that will encourage greater levels of engagement within my entire team while enhancing organizational performance and minimizing retention risk?

Two Ways to Learn from The Past

Experience is not what happens to you;
it's what you do with what happens to you.
—Aldous Huxley

During the 2016 GOP Presidential primaries, potential candidate Jeb Bush was asked a vexing question from a reporter: "Knowing what we know now, would you have made the decision to invade Iraq in 2003?" Bush's answers on this evolved over several days, but I would argue it was the wrong question to ask.

He should have been asked what lessons have been learned from this previous behavior and how do they inform us about making better decisions in the future. David Brooks is an editorial columnist for the New York Times. In his May 19, 2015 column, "Learning from Mistakes," he shares his perspectives on America's decision to go to war in Iraq and states:

"History is an infinitely complex web of causations. To erase mistakes from the past is to obliterate your world now. You can't go back and know then what you know now. You can't step in the same river twice.

So it's really hard to give simple sound-bite answers about past mistakes. The question, would you go back and undo your errors is unanswerable. It's only useful to ask, what wisdom have you learned from your misjudgments that will help you going forward?"

In my work with clients and their teams, I have frequently facilitated discussions that help the group reflect on efforts over the past six months or year to reinforce progress that has been made and gain perspective about how the team continues to develop and progress. It really does help them to focus on how the wisdom of their judgments, not just their misjudgments, has informed them about their continual improvement as a high-performing entity. Here are the two techniques that I use:

Prouds and Sorries: This simple technique is a great way to have a team reflect on all those things they are proud of having accomplished and some things they are sorry they either did not complete or get around to. It's simply a way to create a quick perspective that reinforces the positive but gives voice to those opportunities for improvement. My experience has been that people often focus on what went wrong—the sorries—and are less focused on their accomplishments. When I provide clients their feedback from my 360-degree interviews, where I divide the feedback into pluses (the good stuff) and challenges (the not so good stuff), I often find that my clients will go right to the challenges first. I gently chastise them to go back to the beginning and focus on the positives first.

This "proud and sorry" process asks everyone to identify an accomplishment that the team should be proud of first. I use the "whip" method to go around the room and record one item from each person in succession. If it comes to someone's turn and they don't have an immediate answer, they can pass, and you just keep going until the team runs out of ideas. This technique allows everyone to participate and fosters what is referred to as "piggybacking," where one person's idea creates ideas from others. Once the "prouds" are finished, I repeat the process for the "sorries."

I would suggest that "prouds and sorries" is a great tool for team meetings to generate some positive energy, but it's not really a diagnostic tool in and of itself. For a real diagnosis, I would suggest a more expansive examination of the lessons learned from any significant endeavor or accomplishments over a specific time period.

Lessons Learned: This is a somewhat more formal diagnostic process and generally covers a set of events in a specified time frame. Reviewing the accomplishments relative to a set of predetermined objectives will always be helpful. I suggest this process be facilitated so the participants can fully focus on their reflections. Here are some key elements that make this a successful process:

- **Who:** Be clear about who is invited to participate and ensure that all relevant parties and decision-makers are involved. Too large a group can inhibit effective dialogue. It also helps to suggest that people do some reflection prior to the meeting about the key issues to be discussed. This evaluation exercise is important, so it deserves preparation.

- **What:** Because it is a diagnostic exercise, you should focus on particular outcomes, a set of events or methods that were used to reach an outcome.

- **Where:** This exercise can be done anywhere, but it is critical that enough uninterrupted time be allocated for it. It can be beneficial to conduct the evaluation off-site so distractions can be minimized.

- **Why:** The process is about identifying any "wisdom" that the group can learn from its own activities, especially as it relates to how effectively the team itself operates, not just the outcomes. Working on the business like this is how any group gets better.

- **When:** Pick a point in time when enough of the outcomes from an effort are clear. An annual review should be a minimum.

- **How:** I suggest this process be facilitated and you need to ensure that:
  - Someone is keeping a record of key points;
  - The ground rules for this effort focus not on laying blame but on understanding how decision-making can be improved;
  - The leader uses these efforts to identify and communicate what the lessons learned have been and how these lessons will inform and impact group behavior going forward.

It's important to take time to reflect on and capture the wisdom that our life and business experiences teach us. The process is difficult to do by yourself, but a group activity can be both reassuring and reaffirming.

Ask yourself:

- Do my team and I take the time to reflect on what we've learned and how that can help us make better choices in the future?

- Do we approach such reflection with enough rigor to be sure that we capture the key insights?

- Is the process we engage in one that lifts the mood and spirit of the team?

Five Key Suggestions for Setting Dynamic Goals

We must all suffer from one of two pains: the pain of discipline
or the pain of regret. The difference is discipline weighs ounces
while regret weighs tons.
—Jim Rohn

Another chapter provides some ideas for how to keep your frame of reference in reviewing last year's goal attainment in the proper perspective. Let's focus here on setting goals for the coming year.

Michael Hyatt is a leadership guru (www.michaelhyatt.com) that I follow online. He is a former publishing executive who has been successful in building an online marketing juggernaut from scratch. He recently hosted a goal-setting seminar that I found enlightening and motivating. Here are some key steps he suggested for making progress on your goals. I have added my take on each:

1. Believe you can win. You must have faith that whatever you are undertaking is right for you, your team, your clients and your organization. If you are not confident that achieving this goal will be a positive experience for you, you will not give it the effort you should. Always be sure a goal serves your own "enlightened self-interest." And never hesitate to put yourself first when deciding to engage. The problem arises when your interests are not aligned with everyone else's. Theodore Roosevelt said, "Believe you can and you're halfway there."

2. Get past the past. I don't know anyone who hasn't failed at something. I know I have. But don't let yourself be limited by whatever fears that experience has left you with.

3. Set specific goals. You've probably heard about S.M.A.R.T. Goals: Specific, Measurable, Attainable, Results Oriented and Time Framed. The two most critical aspects here are the Mom Test and the Client Test. The Mom Test says that if you shared the goal you developed with your mom, she would get the gist of what you were saying. This is not about "dumbing it down," it's about clarity! The Client Test says that if you asked the person, customer or team your work was intended to serve, they would get a big smile on their face and say, "Yes, that's exactly what I want!"

4. Know your WHY. I have written about this in my blog posts (http://executivecoachingconcepts.com/what-is-your-why/). Be clear that your goals are in sync with your purpose in the organization and consistent with who you are as a person. Knowing your WHY and that of your role in the organization creates greater alignment and focus.

5. Get started now. Victor Kiam, American entrepreneur, said, "Procrastination is opportunity's assassin." There is never enough time to get everything done, but perfectionism and procrastination can derail any important task. Carve out time for the hard work of setting goals and just do it!

Another insight of Hyatt was that "high achievers know the path becomes clear only when they are in motion." Many years ago my mentor had a sign outside his office that said, "Make it happen— NOW!" This was way before Nike came on the scene, and his point was always do some planning, but don't let the planning become your goal by mistake. There are no perfect plans for any important historical achievement. Get moving and eliminate the stuff that doesn't work— but keep moving! You may not be able to see the end of the path, but the next few steps will become clear.

Fortune magazine has a brief section in each edition called called "The Best Advice I Ever Got." It's always interesting. Several years ago the contributor was Anne Sweeney, co-chair of Disney Media

Networks and president of Disney-ABC Television Group. Anne mentioned that she and her family were strolling around the farmer's market in San Francisco over a long weekend. She said, "As I wandered by this one stall, I looked up and saw a piece of steel that had been etched with a quote. It asked, 'What would you attempt to do if you knew you could not fail?' It literally stopped me in my tracks." She had always wanted to paint and even had the gift of art lessons from her husband. But she worried she wouldn't really be any good. But after that weekend she decided it was time. "...and I decided I would try and govern my life going forward under this principle. So now I paint. It might be good, it might not, but in the end it really doesn't matter. What matters is that you experience it as if you could not fail. It speaks to big dreams, innovation, challenging yourself and pushing to create what's next. It's the kind of advice that makes you take professional risks, too. It's something a lot of members of my team quote back to me."

So as you focus on your goals for the future, ask yourself:

- As I reflect on past goals or make new ones, am I keeping Michael Hyatt's five goal-setting guides in mind?

- Am I moving toward making my goals happen or am I stuck in developing perfect goals?

- What would I attempt to do if I knew I could not fail? What doors does that attitude open for me?

- When my goals are ready, will I share them so I can get the help and support to make them a reality?

THREE SUGGESTIONS FOR REVIEWING GOAL ATTAINMENT

Perfection of means and confusion of goals seem,
in my opinion, to characterize our age.
—ALBERT EINSTEIN

WHETHER YOUR BUSINESS OPERATES on the calendar year or a fiscal year, there is always a time when you must review the year's performance or prepare to do so. It's valuable to see how well you have performed and to prepare for the next year's objectives. How do you build on past success or use that foundation to prepare for the next steps? Oh, and sometimes that review is done to justify what you may be due for bonus considerations. The latter is usually a minor concern for many leaders. Okay, I am just kidding about that.

At my last corporate career stop, I was told I would have a bonus consideration of up to 25 percent of my base pay. When I asked what the performance criteria were, I didn't get a clear answer. The reality was that if the company was profitable, you were on the bonus list and if still employed, you qualified. The old, "Can you fog a mirror?" test. When we got a new CEO, he asked me to develop a goal-setting system to align executive performance and reward people based on that. It was rolled out at the beginning of the year and each participant submitted goals that were reviewed in some depth. Guess what happened? Come November, I got lots of calls from participants asking for copies of their goals so they could prepare for the year-end review. Rather than providing direction, the goals had sat on a shelf. It took a few years for the CEO to use this generous system to enhance performance and align the organization.

Please don't misinterpret. I firmly believe in the positive power of motivating people based on their performance through goals that push performance to new and different levels. But one key problem is that when people engage in reviewing their goals, they can often fall into traps that make this process potentially counterproductive. Dan Sullivan leads The Strategic Coach organization (www.strategiccoach.com), and I was a client of his several years ago. One key concept I learned from that experience was to recognize the various gaps that are part of any goal-setting and review process. Here is how Sullivan represented it:

Gap 1: The distance between where we were (or are) and a future state that is usually a significant leap forward. This is where the idea of "stretch goals" comes from, where you are really trying to push the edge of the envelope. In this graphic, it's also referred to as a horizon, like where you see the sun rise or set.

Gap 2: This is the distance between where you were and where you are now, at the time you are reviewing your goal attainment—either on an annual or quarterly basis. A periodic review is helpful in any group or team to ensure progress is being made on the right things and that efforts are aligned within the team with the broader organization.

Gap 3: This is the distance from your current level of performance to that horizon or stretch level of performance. That definition will need to be reviewed as circumstances develop competitively and based on the changing needs of your business.

Based upon this model, here are three suggestions to consider for reviewing your performance:

1. Avoid the Gap 1 perspective! If you set this as your real expectation, you are setting yourself up for failure. Why? Can you ever travel far enough to actually reach a horizon? No! It's a concept that keeps moving as you move with it. It's like

dangling a carrot out there too far. It's great to have goals that push and stretch you, but keep things realistic. You have to make the vision a reality you can realistically pursue in stages.

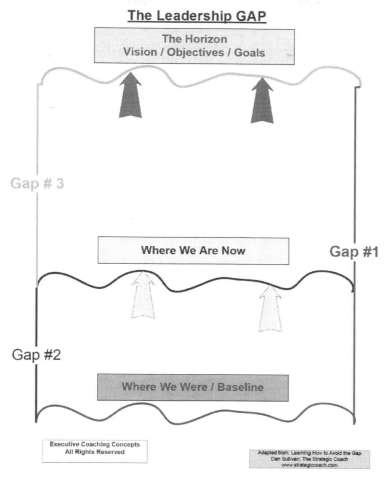

The Leadership GAP

The Horizon
Vision / Objectives / Goals

Gap # 3

Where We Are Now

Gap #1

Gap #2

Where We Were / Baseline

Adapted from: Learning How to Avoid the Gap
Dan Sullivan; The Strategic Coach
www.strategiccoach.com

2. When you reflect on Gap 2, be brutally honest about what you have accomplished and what may have been missed. If you always blow through your goals, some might think you have "sandbagged" the goal process. That means you set targets you

knew were easily attainable based on information you had that others may not have had. This is why regular conversations about goal progress during the year are so critical.

3. Do a "post-mortem" or "lessons learned" on your year. Get your team together and talk about all the positive things that have happened and any disappointments you may share. Usually "prouds" exceed the "sorries," but ensuring that this level of honest reflection is part of your leadership practice sets a great example for everyone.

As you reflect on your team's performance for the year, ask yourself:

• Did we set solid goals that pushed us forward but also kept us on track?

• Have we been honest about how we have been doing and quick to react to the realities along the way?

• Have we celebrated our successes and used our disappointments to refocus as needed?

TIME

INTRO: MAKING TIME YOUR ALLY

One of the key building blocks of being able to manage well is being able to use your time effectively. In today's distracted world, the sheer volume of information that floods our days is enough to drown even a strong swimmer. I am old enough to recall operating in a high-performance corporate environment before the advent of the personal computer, fax machine, email or FedEx. When I came back to my office after a series of meetings, my secretary would often hand me a stack of pink "While You Were Out" phone messages for me to respond to. That's how we got things done.

I have done my best to keep up with technology, but now social media like Twitter, Facebook and a myriad of other instant communication tools can be overwhelming. The amount of information racing around out there is measured in petabytes, which, according to Wikipedia, is 10^{15} bytes, 1,000 terabytes. Just for scale, if you took all the print collections in the Library of Congress and digitized them, it would amount to one terabyte! We are confronted with a huge amount of information overload! To balance the need for focus in this age of outrageous distraction, a good manager and effective leader must exercise increasing discipline.

Two countervailing forces—the time scarcity caused by information overload and the need for time for creative and innovative thinking— create enormous pressure on leaders everywhere. But this also reinforces an important concept—the critical value of pattern recognition. When thinking and doing what you already know and have done successfully, experience enables you to recognize patterns of information and responses that allow you to sort through large volumes of information to make effective leadership decisions. If not for these patterns and your ability to recognize them, you would be relearning with each new problem. But if you apply those same patterns of thought in a situation that is unique or that reflects rapidly changing trends, you are at risk of applying old solutions to new problems.

How do you find the time for yourself and your teams to analyze, strategize, plan and prioritize? The bad news is that none of these things can be done at breakneck pace. So you need an effective filter for looking at how you spend your time and then seek ways to reallocate it to be better prepared for these challenges. To start, I ask my clients to refer to the following model from Stephen Covey's book, *First Things First*.

COVEY MODEL

	URGENT	NON URGENT
IMPORTANT	**B** • Crises • Pressing problems • Deadline-driven projects, meetings, preparations	**A** • Preparation • Prevention • Values clarification • Planning • Relationship building • True re-creation • Empowerment
NOT IMPORTANT	**C** • Interruptions, some phone calls • Some mail, some reports • Some meetings • Many pressing matters • Many popular activities	**D** • Trivia, busywork • Some phone calls • Time wasters • "Escape" activities • Irrelevant mail • Excessive TV

Adapted from First Things First, Steven R. Covey, A. Roger Merrill, Rebecca R. Merrill, Fireside Press

Let's examine how this model relates to leadership responsibilities.

Urgency: Simply stated, some things have a time sensitivity that creates an immediate need for action. Urgency is usually a relative term, depending on the financial significance of needed actions, the initiator of the actions (such as your boss) or opportunities to be taken advantage of.

Importance: Some things are more important than others. When you reflect on the goals for yourself and your team, priorities emerge. The relative importance may have to do with the people involved, the financial implications of the work you're doing and any current work processes or improvements you have undertaken. As a leader, you must consider what's important to you, those who work for you and teammates across the organization. You can get pressed into service because of your experience, knowledge of the organization or your communication style. People want to take advantage of what you have to offer, but the energy you expend on those tasks may diminish the time you can spend on your direct goals and those of the team that works for you directly. This dilemma is often referred to as an opportunity cost, and you must weigh it carefully in terms of your performance and that of your team versus your opportunity to build, maintain and enhance relationships across the organization. So when it comes to evaluating importance, you have to be sure you're focused on your priorities.

Not Important/Non-Urgent: You may occasionally play a few online games, view YouTube videos or communicate via Facebook or Twitter with your friends, but Covey says that effective people spend no more than three percent of their time in this quadrant.

Important/Urgent: These are the key, usually time-sensitive, responsibilities that you must attend to regularly as well as crisis situations that inevitably arise from time to time. Your ability to reliably produce in this quadrant was critical to your career development. You showed yourself to be dependable, creative and cooperative in making things happen. As markets change and responsibilities shift, and the scope of your efforts ebb and flow over the years, your experience allows you to be more efficient in responding to the many challenges that come your way. It's where pattern recognition pays off.

Not Important/Urgent: In the course of a normal day, you may be deluged with requests and demands on your time. I have had many clients bemoan that their days are stacked with inefficient and ineffective meetings, but their presence has been requested. Some of the face time in these meetings is part of the political price you pay for being in any organization. Interruptions—whether they are in-person, phone calls, email or texts—can barrage you in those limited times that you try to grab for yourself. It's critical to remember that requests for your time or attention may not seem to rise to the level of what's important for you, but they are to the requesters. As a leader you must establish boundaries and communicate clearly to others how you are going to spend your time and give others access to you. I advocate careful communication to establish these boundaries and a steely resolve to maintain them.

Important/Non-Urgent: This is the holy grail of leadership opportunity, the critical time that I hope you are zealously seeking, where you can engage in critical leadership activities that enhance the possibilities for success for you, your team and your organization. This area is where you are carving out time for:

- Planning
- Preparing
- Building relationships and a strong network
- Clarifying and reinforcing the organizational values that reflect the culture you're trying to support.

These are the higher order leadership responsibilities that cannot be well executed in "crunch time." I have seen high-performing organizations where senior leaders are at the beck and call of the CEO and have to drop everything and respond to what can seem like capricious requests. The organization succeeds in spite of itself, but it's neither a happy place nor one capable of reaching its full potential. Respect for the investment of time in these critical tasks is lost in many organizations, but not in the most effective and highest performing ones.

Thoreau said, "Nothing can be more useful to a man than a determination not to be hurried." Of course, these words came from a man who decided to live a portion of his life in the woods by Walden Pond. That would certainly limit the distractions that are a part of our life today. There is inherent logic in Covey's Important/Not Urgent quadrant, and if you have experienced the development of great ideas that were brought to fruition, you long for the heady atmosphere of achieving such goals again. If that's true, then why don't you allocate more time and energy to making such things happen?

There is a very simple answer to that question and it's called human nature. Built into us is a fight-or-flight syndrome that is fueled by the adrenaline rush that a challenging situation creates. The adrenaline causes us to become hypersensitive to our surroundings and speed up our thinking. Those primal instincts have ensured our survival through the eons, and the "buzz" of that adrenaline rush is addictive. We are not a patient species. We know we need more time to plan and create new and better things, but we are addicted to doing things quickly, so we can check off a to-do list.

Why the Clock Always Wins

In the struggle to make time an ally rather than an adversary, we wonder why the clock always seems to win, why we never seem to have enough time for the things that matter. Here are five reasons the clock always wins:

- Failure to know where the time actually goes
- A lack of alignment to common goals
- Too many ineffective meetings
- The inability to delegate effectively
- The failure to productively consolidate what little discretionary time we have

Knowing Where the Time Goes: I learned a long time ago that you can measure almost everything. You all have calendars that you keep, so there is a ready source of insight about how you are actually spending your time. The key is to spend some impactful time analyzing that treasure trove. The next chapter, **To Exploit Your Time Resources, Do A Time Bucket Analysis** will provide a template for doing just that.

Lack of Alignment to Common Goals: Yogi Berra, the great Yankee baseball catcher, manager and philosopher once said, "If you don't know where you're going, you might not get there."

I have been amazed at how many organizations do not know how to set effective goals that drive results, increase focus and align energies to make the most productive use of everyone's time. To an extent, this is an organizational discipline that distinguishes the most successful companies from the also-rans. It's a part of the corporate culture that creates alignment across key functions to achieve the organization's purpose and promise.

The discipline to stay focused on goals is daunting because it's a lot more fun to just grab after the next "shiny object" or program of the month. Most people have been exposed to the concept of SMART goals—specific, measurable, attainable, results oriented and within a time frame. But not many organizations actually adhere to that framework and have the rigor and discipline to ensure that everyone plays by the same rules. It takes an effective leader to create a review process that creates a focus throughout the organization to ensure that people are all rowing the boat in the same direction as efficiently as possible.

Too Many Ineffective Meetings: The adage, "I'd be rich if I had a dollar for all the time I waste in meetings," is one I hear with numbing frequency. I was conducting a meeting with 11 senior technical contributors when their frustration with the organizational demands placed on them for attendance at so many meetings just boiled over in my presence. Many of these people indicated that they were trapped in meetings all day and the only time for them to get their own work done was early in the morning, in the evening and on weekends. I have seen this situation in many organizations. It isn't that getting together to exchange ideas, create alignment and work on the business is not valuable, but there needs to be rigorous discipline in running meetings efficiently.

Earlier in my career I was asked to work with the head of engineering and the head of quality assurance to design a total quality program for the RCA Consumer Electronics Division. I learned a lot about the Japanese total quality programs, many of which were designed by Americans who found a ready audience in the Japanese manufacturing world. A key element of these programmatic successes was the discipline and purpose in how they ran meetings.

Program management and the use of agile technologies in many software development shops reflect disciplined efforts to achieve better results. But if you do not operate in technical or engineering disciplines, some basic rules of meeting management can help you make the best use of everyone's time. It doesn't matter which model you choose, but make some decisions and stick to them. If I learned anything during my immersion into the world of TQM, it's that you can measure anything. You just need to have desire and discipline.

Below are key questions to guide an effective meeting. If you can focus on these elements consistently, you will have better meetings.

- Who absolutely needs to be in this meeting? Can we let people opt out if they need to be there for only a few minutes?
- What is the purpose of the meeting? What would a good outcome look like?
- What is our agenda and have we allocated the right amount of time based on the importance of each agenda item? Who's helping to keep us on track?
- Do we have summaries of action items for each meeting? If not, why even bother to show up?
- Who is responsible for follow-up tracking for all agreements and initiatives that come out of any meeting?

The Inability to Delegate: If there's one thing any leader should avoid, it's a bottleneck. Managers must learn how to let go and delegate effectively. I have had interesting discussions with highly qualified technical people who have management opportunities that initially overwhelm them. Part of the cause is very simple—it's the fear of losing the currency of your technical or operational abilities. It's not really about delegating or not delegating at this point because these individuals refuse to let go. They want to stay involved and they do it for reasons that I call the myths of ineffective delegation:

- No one can do it as well as I can.
- It would take me too long to explain; I can do it quicker.
- I don't trust them (like I do myself).
- I can't afford to let them fail (because of the blowback on me).
- I don't want to let go. I love this stuff!

What we need to remember is that there are elements of truth in myths. But there comes a point of diminishing returns, when the manager who becomes the bottleneck burns out, frustrating everybody else along the way.

Failure to Consolidate Discretionary Time: Although many people lament the fact that they have little time for doing their own work beyond spending time in meetings, it takes a concerted effort to be able to think differently about time priorities and come up with creative and innovative ideas in the workplace.

If you do not find a way to break free from being an adrenaline junkie at work, you will never find the courage to consolidate what limited discretionary time you might have to get your creative juices flowing effectively. Some companies sponsor weeks where everyone is supposed to take on pet projects to keep those juices flowing. But you will never complete a project that demands six hours of effort in random 15-minute increments. It may take courage to block out that time, but it will be worth it.

Ways to Beat the Clock

So if you want to make time an ally rather than an adversary, here are some key actions that taken together can provide a head start toward the free time you need to really shine as a manager and a leader:

• Make your meetings count. Be absolutely disciplined about the ones that you lead and run.

• Limit your meetings to 45 to 50 minutes. You need time to get from one meeting to the other, to organize and prepare for the next meeting and take a break. Have somebody call time every 15 minutes because time pressure works to your advantage.

- Not all meetings need to last an hour. Try scheduling things in 30-minute increments but ending after 25. It forces people to be prepared and focused.

- Allocate certain hours for returning calls and email. Schedule hour or half-hour increments during the day to stay caught up. Give yourself time to do your work.

- If you have an assistant, learn how to use him/her to screen your calls and email and to help keep your files and appointments in order. Let your assistants be facilitators of your time rather than gatekeepers. Empower them.

- Reconsider your "open door" policy. Avoid the continuous partial attention disorder that occurs when people can just walk in and disrupt your thought process because they caught you in your office. I'm not saying don't be accessible, but put boundaries around your availability so that you can give somebody your absolute full attention when you are speaking with them. People may seem miffed when you try to implement such a change, but they will learn to appreciate the fact that you are fully present when they are working with you.

- Decide to become an excellent delegator. Empower your people by ensuring they have the clarity needed to take on responsibility.

- Do an office purge quarterly or semiannually to get rid of the stuff you meant to read or do something with but now is just in the way.

- Since everybody is a working manager or leader these days, you have a right to be selfish about your time, up to a point. Don't hesitate to say that you are not available if somebody interrupts you, but be willing to set up a time that is convenient for both of you.

My favorite things in life don't cost any money. It's really clear that the most precious resource we all have is time.
—STEVE JOBS

To Exploit Your Time Resources, Do a Time Bucket Analysis

*The biggest waste of time is to do well
something that we need not do at all.*
—Gretchen Rubin

Let's go back to the client of mine who was asked to take the helm of a new brokerage branch that combined three existing branches in a major metropolitan area. Its design would make it the new benchmark across the national platform. This branch manager is also a member of a successful team within the branch that deals mainly with high-net-worth clients. She has been recognized nationally as being one of the top branch managers in the country across financial services firms.

As the planning for the actual consolidation drew near, I asked my client how she was going to adjust her work efforts to accomplish all that was going to be required in the new role. I suggested she do a "time bucket analysis," and she identified the top five to seven key areas where her time should be going. She then tracked her actual time to see where it went. My client realized very quickly that she had a potentially difficult issue on her hands.

As a senior female leader in a predominantly male industry, she was very much in demand for participating in diversity and women-focused initiatives in the firm. And she enjoyed her work on those efforts. However, when she counted the amount of time she gave these efforts, both within the firm and in the community, she realized she had a problem. She had let it get away from her. With the shifting demands on her time for the new branch office, she would not be able to maintain the same level of commitment, regardless of the personal interest and the intrinsic rewards she enjoyed from such initiatives.

A time bucket analysis involves examining areas where your work time is spent. Here's a list of buckets for a senior technical vice president of a leading cable company in the United States:

- **Team Management/Development:** Reviews, HR, team-building, interviews, classes
- **Project Management:** Staff meetings, prioritization meetings, my boss' staff, my boss' boss' staff, cross-functional meetings, legal meetings
- **Research and Development:** Lab time, research hours, vendor tech calls
- **Industry News and Networking:** Vendor sales calls, conferences, contact calls, updating contacts
- **Intra-Company Development:** Meetings and calls regarding projects outside the scope of the high-speed data product
- **Write Code/Quality Assurance/Others' Work:** Coding and quality assurance hours, and bug scrubs

Years ago, I read an article in *Fortune* magazine about the CEO of Starbucks. I developed this chart to show how he said he spent his time.

Time Chart Starbucks CEO

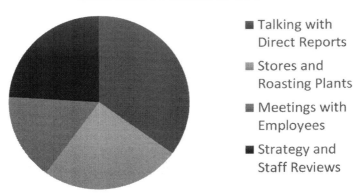

- Talking with Direct Reports
- Stores and Roasting Plants
- Meetings with Employees
- Strategy and Staff Reviews

If you end up with more than seven buckets, you are in danger of creating a task list. Your time analysis should be much simpler. Once you have determined your buckets, ask yourself:

- How much of your time do you intend to spend in each bucket? Assign a percentage to each.
- Start now and begin to track actual time spent versus your intentions. Where are the GAPs?
- Where did you spend more time than you intended?
- Where did you spend less time? Why?
- This is a good time to consider how the rhythms of the year influence how your time is spent. Monthly, quarterly and annual meetings and reports should not pop up and surprise you. Plan to give yourself more time to prepare. Include such projects in how you intend to use your time.
- What's sucking up your time, taking more than you had allotted or think it should?
- Renegotiate, delegate and track your time. Find time for planning and preparation and get out of things you know are no longer a high priority.
- If you don't measure it, you can't improve it. Have your assistant help keep tabs on your time after you explain your priorities.

The client I introduced you to earlier let the leaders of groups and task forces she was on know that she would discontinue her involvement or scale it back. She got out in front of the issue and communicated on her terms. That way no one was left hanging, and she did not suffer by disappointing herself or others by failing to attend. She has no regrets about her decision to focus on her priorities.

You are the only one who can control the majority of the time you spend on your duties.

Ask yourself:

- Do the choices I make regarding how my time is spent reflect the very best investment for me, my team and the organization? (And it should be in that order!)

- Am I willing to be disciplined about identifying where I am out of balance in the use of my time?

- Can I renegotiate or delegate to get to a better balance?

"Chunking" Your Time—A Simple Model for Increased Impact

Time is the coin of your life. It is the only coin you have,
and only you can determine how it will be spent.
Be careful lest you let other people spend it for you.
—Carl Sandburg

A foundational element of my coaching work is to have clients review how they spend their time as leaders so they can make choices that will allow them to focus on what is truly important, rather than get sucked into what I call the "busyness vortex" of their work world. Since many of my clients see their time consumed by back-to-back meetings, I often suggest they schedule blocks of time for planning, building relationships and other key leadership duties.

A client of mine recently gave me a book entitled *Give and Take*, by Adam Grant.[17] It is a richly researched book by the youngest tenured professor at the University of Pennsylvania's Wharton School of Business. Grant discusses the different styles of interacting with others that lead to the greatest level of success in business and life. I'd like to describe his theory in brief and tell you what he says about a key choice for managing time that will help anyone, especially leaders, greatly enhance their impact, effectiveness and satisfaction in their current roles.

Givers, Matchers and Takers

Grant divides people into three categories. The first is "givers," who tend to focus on helping others selflessly, without any strings attached. The second group is called "matchers," and they look at human interactions with a *quid pro quo* mentality. Matchers are willing to help but have a keen eye for what's in it for them before they will engage. "Takers" are individuals who are mostly concerned for themselves. They need to ensure that they get theirs regardless of the effects on others. Takers may or may not be effective Machiavellians, but they are frequently narcissists.

You might consider which of the three you might be. I am sorry, but I have no diagnostic for that. What's interesting is how well Grant can take a sociological/psychological perspective about behavior and demonstrate both the impact and the effectiveness of each style. For instance, his studies show that givers perform about 68 percent better than matchers or takers over time. So here, I'll concentrate on givers as leaders and how they can increase their impact by using their time better.

The Downside of Being a Giver

Grant is clear that like all strengths carried to an extreme, there are potential downsides to being a giver. Selfless givers can actually give too much over a period of time and suffer burnout and exhaustion. Selfless givers are constantly helping their colleagues solve problems and they do it in a way that Grant refers to as "sprinkling." In other words, they are reactive and give their time at the expense of their own needs and work. For instance, sprinklers may find much of their days are taken up with reacting to issues or responding to requests so that the only time they have for their own work is after hours.

This self-sacrifice is okay from time to time, but it reaches diminishing results quickly if it becomes the norm. In my work with a group of senior technical leaders in a major national cable company, I saw this pattern play out regularly. These fellows did not have the time to plan, think and prepare. Ignoring your own needs is also ineffective in building relationships and influencing others.

Chunking Your Time

Grant contrasts the sprinklers with "chunkers," another subset of givers. A chunker creates dedicated windows of time for interactions, planning and thinking. He uses the example of a group of engineers charged with a radical new design for a printer. These were highly talented engineers, but they had never delivered a new design on time or on or under budget. The group made a commitment to chunking their time during this product development cycle. During this dedicated time, coworkers knew they should avoid interrupting the team and respect these windows.

In one study, two thirds of engineers who adopted a chunking time model reported above average productivity. Instead of reacting to whatever came their way whenever it came, they could be focused because they knew they had time set aside in their schedules to do their own work. They also delivered a new printer that was 10 percent less expensive and did it on time and on budget.

Grant was able to demonstrate that givers, what he refers to as "otherish" givers, are incredibly more effective and satisfied in their work than selfless givers, matchers or takers. The difference between selfless and otherish givers is that the otherish givers are helpful to others but not at an expense to themselves. They find a balanced method to accomplish their own goals and help others as well.

Increasing Your Impact and Productivity

The biggest challenge in shifting from being a selfless giver is the willingness to ask for help in becoming better at chunking your time. Often organizational and cultural norms prevent immediate changes. How much time each week do you have for planning, preparing and communicating proactively with those you want to influence and ensuring that each member of your team is as engaged as they should be?

A modest modification to your expectations of being infinitely available to your team can actually produce greater overall productivity and greater satisfaction for you as a leader. You have to find ways to block time on your calendar and have others adhere to your new boundaries. Consider how you will communicate the changes to your team, your boss and other people with whom you interact regularly. Many people will admire your making this choice, and the grumbling will abate when others see improved results and a more satisfied you.

Ask yourself:

- Do I feel like I am caught in the busyness vortex at work?

- If I am a giver, am I swept up in the current infinite availability mindset that requires me to respond to any issue that arises almost immediately?

- Have I considered blocking off time to get some key, higher level work done during regular business hours?

- Am I willing to allocate some "me" time on my calendar and see how that works for a month?

- If so, how will I inform others of my new practice and ask them to respect this boundary I am setting?

Take Time to Work "ON" the Business—Three Key Questions for Gaining Control

Time management is an oxymoron. Time is beyond our control,
and the clock keeps ticking regardless of how we lead our lives.
Priority management is the answer to maximizing the time we have.
—John C. Maxwell.

In team support work that I do, I frequently see teams that are so busy chasing all the "stuff" that is the basis of their revenues or goals—what I call working "IN" the business—that they never find time to consistently and thoroughly work "ON" their business to improve HOW they do WHAT they do. Working "ON" the business includes the many HOWs of managing the day to day flow of the efforts of everybody on the team.

Russell Bishop wrote an interesting book on this subject, *Workarounds That Work: How to Conquer Anything That Stands in Your Way at Work*, in which he asked, "What could you do that would make a difference in your job that requires no one's approval, cooperation, support or agreement other than your own?"[18] In his book, Bishop shares this model about all the stuff we have to deal with and suggests that when working "ON" your business, control what you can control.

Bishop defines each element as follows:

- **Control.** The inner circle contains all those things that you can control, where you have the positional and personal power to make decisions all on your own.
- **Influence.** The second layer is about those areas of performance where you may be able to have impact but are dependent on the approval, cooperation, support or agreement of others.

- **Respond.** The outer layer represents everything else that happens in response to what happens around us. We just react or respond, like dressing appropriately based upon the day's weather forecast.

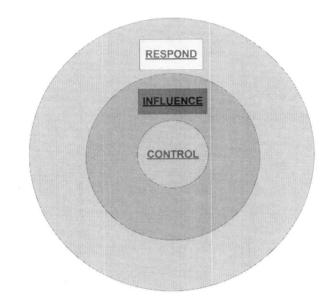

What resonated with me about this model is that our biggest opportunity—if we make time to work on it—is to improve as much as possible all elements of our own work processes and those of our team. If you can consistently improve what you can control, you will be able to influence other things. If you are responding repeatedly to things that force you to work around inefficient or ineffective processes or procedures that you could improve if you invested the time to do so, your pains are self-inflicted.

Three Questions to Gain Control

Bishop challenges his readers by claiming that as much as 20 percent of what's done need not be done anymore. He suggests that you review all your current tasks and projects and then ask these three questions about each item you list:

1. Who needs this done?
2. Why do they need it?
3. What difference will it make?

You must be committed to taking the time to thoughtfully review what's on everyone's plate. Take the time to do this with all key members of the staff. Carefully record your decisions and determine how you will communicate the decisions taken by the team. Your team will appreciate that you know how to gain control and are committed to ensuring that the team consistently is focused on what matters most. When the organization shifts focus or direction, always be ready to ask what should we continue to do, what do we need to start doing and, most important, what should we stop doing?

As you consider this, ask yourself these questions:

- Do I help my team reflect on what we can do to control our workload and workflow?

- Can doing this assist me in becoming more influential in managing our contributions to the organization?

- Can I use this effort to provide opportunities for members of my team to step up and lead as well?

- Lastly, and most importantly, am I afraid to step up and suggest we stop doing things that do not matter anymore?

SEVEN WAYS TO BEAT THE CLOCK

Time is the most valuable thing a man can spend.
—THEOPHRASTUS

As each year hurtles to its conclusion, most people reflect on what they've accomplished and what will fall into the category of "good intentions." Making the best use of time will always be a challenge. Consider some things you can do to better prepare for making an even better use of your time.

1. Make meeting times count.
The bane of existence for the majority of my corporate clients is how their days are filled with back-to-back meetings. Little energy is expended to ensure that meetings are well run, productive and continually advancing whatever project or purpose they are intended to support. Strategically, you can stop going to meetings when you're not sure of the purpose or the need for your attendance or you can send a delegate in your place if you traditionally have found specific meetings to be unproductive. Please see the next chapter, **Eight Questions to Improve Meeting Productivity**, to learn more about how to run effective meetings.

2. Allocate certain hours for returning calls or email.
I don't know how many email or calls you get in a given day, but I have many clients who receive in excess of 200 emails a day. The default for keeping on track with managing such a deluge is usually working on it at night, early in the morning or on the weekends. An alternative would be to allocate one or two hours a day, even if it's in 30-minute increments, to respond to the most pressing email or

urgent calls. The key is you must protect your time and let people know why you are shutting your door and focusing.

3. If you have an assistant, learn how to use him/her.

Not everyone who reads this will have an assistant who works directly for them or that they share. But when such talent is available, it's important to learn how to use it effectively. Have them route your calls for you, set up meetings and manage your calendar and assist with your filing and follow-up. Assistants can also screen email to help you prioritize the use of your response time for the most critical items.

4. Reconsider your "open-door" policy.

Some people pride themselves on being infinitely available to their team and coworkers. An open-door policy reinforces what I call the "continuous partial attention disorder." People drop in and interrupt you when it's convenient for them, making you uncomfortable with asking them to come back later. You probably have little discretionary time in your calendar to begin with, and by enabling others to interrupt you at their leisure, you can be sure that your productivity will be affected negatively. You may have to remind people to respect that you are working when you have your door closed but that it is okay to pop in when it's open.

5. Quarterly office "stuff" purges.

The Japanese have a custom of "*kure*," meaning everyone spends time cleaning out files and reading materials for a clean sweep for the coming year. I have spent time with clients to assist them in office "stuff" overhauls, uncluttering their work areas and files from materials they have inherited or accumulated, often over years. It's important to have discipline in doing this. If you intended to read something but it sat for six months, it's probably no longer relevant. Get things filed away where anyone can find them. Make this an annual event for your team, but remember to have adequate trash receptacles to recycle or dispose of whatever you choose. This clean sweep provides a psychological lift for a "clean" attack on today's challenges. I think a "mini-kure" is in order each quarter to unclutter and put what's important in focus.

6. Learn to delegate with boundaries.

I have developed my own model for helping leaders and managers think through three levels of delegation that are options. The key is for the person delegating to be absolutely clear about which of the three levels of delegation they intend and to ensure that the person they are delegating to is clear as well. It's all about expectations and boundaries.

- **A Steel Chain:** In this scenario, the delegator is unclear about how a project or task will develop. There are unknowns, but you realize you need to get started and you need help. You are figuratively linked as if by a steel chain, ankle to ankle, as you gain clarity about the project design and parameters.

- **A Rubber Band:** Here the project is loosely connected to the delegator, meaning that from time to time he or she may need to pull it back to revisit progress, parameters and expectations that are probably solidifying but still in a state of flux.

- **A Thread:** This situation occurs when the delegator has total clarity about the goals and boundaries of the project and also has a high level of confidence that the individual put in charge is competent to execute. The delegator may request follow-up and notice about project completion or may be just fine with letting it go entirely unless a problem arises. Of course, no delegator wants to be surprised instead of having the opportunity to collaborate or assist in overcoming such problems.

Even if you start with a steel chain, you should progress along the continuum until there is no question between you and your delegatees about your expectations for working on tasks or projects until you agree it is complete. Then you will have learned how to fully delegate tasks within set boundaries.

7. Empower your employees, within boundaries.

Empowerment can be like a yo-yo, and it can be both good and bad. If a person is empowered, they know just what to do to accomplish a task. You can truly say, "**Y**ou're **O**n **Y**our **O**wn" and let them run with it. Otherwise it is really like a yo-yo—it's your task and now it's mine again; it's your task and now it's mine again. It takes a lot of time and familiarity with your staff to find a level of comfort in having them be truly empowered. They will appreciate the autonomy and sense of accomplishment they derive from "owning" certain responsibilities. But by being clear about the limits or boundaries in the exercise of their duties, you will make life easier for everyone and get things off your plate with a sense of confidence. If you feel like you are struggling to see what boundaries you can set on various things, start with the limits your boss has set for you.

Ask yourself:

- What can I do to take better control of my time resources?

- Do I know how to delegate and empower others?

- Am I brave enough to take a stand against wasteful meeting time?

EIGHT QUESTIONS TO INCREASE MEETING PRODUCTIVITY

*If you had to identify, in one word, the reason why
the human race has not achieved, and never will achieve,
its full potential, that word would be "meetings."*
—DAVE BARRY

Many of the senior leaders that I serve complain about the number of meetings they are asked to attend. Days can be consumed by one meeting after the other so there is little time for their real work. Now don't get me wrong, I know a lot of work goes on in meetings, and meetings have the potential to be valuable sources for organizational accomplishment. I often observe my clients in meeting settings to provide them some feedback on their leadership and communication styles. When I broaden my focus to what is actually going on with most participants, here are a few observations I've made:

- In many project-status meetings, people do not pay attention to what's going on unless they are speaking or preparing to speak.

- It is not uncommon to see other members of a management team answering email or texts on their laptops, tablets or phones while others are speaking.

- Meetings are usually scheduled in one hour increments, one right after the other. When do people have time to go to the bathroom or check their phone for calls or email without affecting the next meeting they are attending?

- One aspect of organizational culture has to do with the nature of what is considered late. It's not unusual for people to show up anywhere from five to 20 minutes late. Either everyone else's time is wasted by getting late-comers up to speed or the people who are late never really know what happened.

- If there are 10 people in a meeting and you ask each of them what was accomplished in that meeting, you will get a variety of responses. This lack of clarity and consistency reflects poorly on the meeting leader.

Some people are skilled at the art of meeting management. People who have been trained in project management or Six Sigma Total Quality systems realize that effective meeting management is a critical part of getting the work done well and efficiently. Unfortunately, such skills are often not used or accepted outside those disciplines.

Last year I surveyed the 10 members of a Leadership Learning Lab (a group training program I offer) about their meeting management experience. These individuals were senior technical leaders and most had post-graduate degrees from some of the best technical universities in the country. These were highly influential individuals not only in their organization but also within their industry. In our first meeting, after we had been together only about three hours, several key issues bubbled up and their general level of frustration was high. A key concern was that their days were consumed by one meeting after another, and time for planning, preparation, relationship building and reflection was available to them only after hours. They were frustrated and burned out, dealing with an organizational norm they felt powerless to challenge. We were able to get that meeting back on track, and on my next visit I asked each of the 10 members of the Leadership Learning Lab to complete a short survey about their meeting management experience in their company. Here are some of the key takeaways:

- People average 6.5 meetings a day and each meeting was about 50 minutes long.

- Twenty-five percent of meetings had no visible or appointed leader and 40 percent had no clear purpose, much less an agenda.

- Sixty percent of the time sufficient time was not allocated to the most important topics.

- Next steps were clearly articulated based on the discussion only 34 percent of the time.

- When asked how much more productive they individually could be if meetings were run better, the answer was 31 percent more productive. They were limited to no more than 50 percent, assuming that the other 50 percent of meeting time was reasonably productive.

Each of these participants had a compensation package of salary, bonus, long-term incentives and benefits that exceeded $200,000 per year, and that is a conservative figure. If you consider that a potentially 31 percent improvement in productivity was possible just for these 10 technical leaders, their organization would reap a benefit of more than $600,000 per year if meetings were improved. And that is for only 10 people out of more than 50,000 employees!

You could supply your own horror stories about meetings that were poorly run, ineffective and a complete waste of time. The reality is that the way organizations tolerate such weak standards for meeting effectiveness is a reflection of organizational culture. And even healthy organizations that are proud of their culture will tolerate poor behavior in meetings. The reasons for that are complex, so let's just zero in on a few key meeting management expectations that you should insist on for any meeting that you lead or can influence.

Key questions for any meeting:

1. Who is responsible for the effectiveness of this meeting?
2. Why are we here?
3. What do we need to accomplish in the time we have?
4. What would a good outcome look like?
5. How will we keep ourselves on task? How do we avoid tangents and distractions?
6. Are we clear about who does what next?
7. Where can we find the summary of this meeting?
8. When do we need to follow up? Or do we?

It is my belief that if the leader of any meeting stays true to these questions of meeting management, you will greatly increase the productivity and satisfaction of each member of the team. I would also suggest that you institute 25-minute and 50-minute long meetings and have someone call out when there are 10 and 5 minutes left to go in each meeting to ensure prompt wrap-up times.

Ask yourself:

- If I'm frustrated about all the time I waste in meetings, am I willing to do something about it?

- Am I worried about what others would say if I institute these modest changes in the meetings that I lead?

- If I'm frustrated and not worried about what others might say, why don't I start tomorrow?

TO ENHANCE PRODUCTIVITY, STOP DOING SOMETHING!

*Besides the noble art of getting things done, there is
the noble art of leaving things undone. The wisdom of life
consists in the elimination of nonessentials.*
—LIN YUTANG

THE FULL EMPLOYMENT RATE WAS considered to be 94 percent back when I was in college. That means that 6 percent of the workforce being unemployed was considered "normal." By the time the dot-com boom hit its peak in 2000, full employment was thought to be closer to 96 percent. This may not seem like a big difference, but it is millions of jobs and reflected the hubris of the times.

Economists today say the full employment rate in the United States is between 94.5 and 95 percent. Our country may be approaching a real tightness in the labor market. As competition for employees grows, companies will feel the pressure to hire and retain staff. One of the ways to attract and keep employees is to ensure they feel properly challenged by their work and that they are truly productive, not just busy. In the post-baby boomer age, people won't stay where they think their time is wasted. Finding ways to retain employees will be critical to success.

Companies must continue to improve productivity. During the last several decades significant investments in software and systems have assisted in that. But what's missing is an ongoing reevaluation of all the work that's being done. If you become more efficient at doing things that really shouldn't be done anymore, you are squandering any productivity gains.

Who gives someone permission to stop doing something that is no longer needed? And who decides that it isn't needed any longer? In today's environment, employees seem fearful of speaking up about these issues. So to increase productivity, managers should find ways to stop doing at least five percent of what's currently being done.

In a 40-hour work week, that means you'll be finding two hours per week per employee to do things that are more important, to stay more organized or to plan and prepare for new opportunities.

Here is a step-by-step plan for doing just that:

• Announce that you are asking everyone to eliminate the bottom five percent of their tasks so they can focus on more important things.

• Ask everyone to identify three tasks to eliminate, put it in writing and bring it to a meeting to discuss it with the whole team. If your team is too large, you may have to break it up into groups, but it is important that everyone hear other ideas about what can be eliminated. It may encourage different or new thinking on the part of others when they hear these ideas. That's called "piggybacking."

• Have team members review their lists out loud. Others may ask for them to clarify the tasks they have identified, but they are not allowed to argue with them about whether or not it can be eliminated at this point. Have each member of the team identify which of those three tasks they feel strongest about and would commit to. Do not debate. Just get things on the table.

• Now have each member of the team repeat the key task they want to eliminate and have the group rate it as follows:

  • "Duh!" Of course we should stop doing that.
  • Probably no problem, but there may be a couple things to check on first.
  • Since there have been some concerns raised, let's put that on the "to be considered" list for later.
  • No, we can't stop that, and here's why . . . .

- If a suggested change is rejected based on the collective wisdom of the team, have the team member go to the next task on the list.
- Combine the list of the "duhs" and "probably no problem ..." tasks and send that list to the entire team.
- Make a separate list of the "to be considered" tasks for later review. At this point, everyone commits to trying to eliminate the task(s) they have identified.
- The manager must reinforce that anyone who runs into a problem or an unintended consequence of eliminating certain tasks should inform the manager as soon as practical.
- Have a brief meeting after two weeks to report in on any things that have been learned about stopping these tasks. Talk about the time that's been freed up and any concerns that may exist.
- After a month, review the status of each task that has been stopped and see if any adjustments need to be made. Ask each member of the team what lessons have been learned from the exercise and record the responses.

Saving everybody two hours a week is a reasonable and modest effort that should free up time for more important tasks. It may also identify other process bottlenecks that exist and require further study. Once you believe this exercise has been productive, repeat as needed, but commit to doing so at least once a year.

Ask yourself:

- Do I need anyone's permission to do this with my team?

- Am I willing to follow through on things once we've started?

- Can I get members of my team to help track progress?

THE DILEMMA OF
"UNDER-MANAGING" AND TIME

*The simple act of paying positive attention to people
has a great deal to do with productivity.*
—TOM PETERS

AS A LEADER, IT CAN OFTEN SEEM like you are running into the stream from a powerful water hose and to succeed, you just have to run faster and faster to keep up. What can get crowded out is the time to plan so you can stay ahead of all the challenges that come your way. What does this situation cost you, your team and your organization? Most of us have felt this way from time to time, but how do we break this vicious cycle?

Some recent research on this particular topic can serve as a model for evaluating how you spend your time and will reinforce that making time for reflection and preparation greatly enhances your productivity and accelerates the wisdom you obtain from your leadership experiences.

Bruce Tulgan is the head of Rainmaker Thinking (www. Rainmaker Thinking.com). His recent white paper, "The Under-management Epidemic Report 2014: Ten Years Later"[19] states that in 10 years of tracking how engaged employees are, he has found that managers are not consistently engaged in providing supervisory authority on what he refers to as the "management basics." These management basics include setting performance expectations, providing support and guidance, monitoring and measuring performance, providing regular feedback about performance and allocating rewards in proportion to actual performance. Tulgan maintains that employees are not engaged because managers do not regularly practice these management basics.

The costs of this under-management epidemic are:

- Unnecessary problems occur.
- Small problems that should have been solved with relative ease instead get worse before they are identified and solved.
- Resources are squandered, and managers and employees spend time salvaging resources and acquiring substitute resources.
- Employees fail to do tasks according to established best practices for extended periods of time before anybody realizes it.
- Low performers are not identified or held accountable.
- Mediocre performers often mistake themselves for high performers.
- High performers suffer diminished morale and are more likely to leave their jobs voluntarily.
- Managers spend more time performing lower level tasks that should have been delegated to a direct-report.

I encourage you to visit Tulgan's site and review his findings in depth. The key question you need to ask yourself, especially if any combination of these eight elements of this under-management epidemic is visible in your workplace, is what's the primary cause? According to Tulgan's article, "The vast majority of managers still cite 'lack of time' (due mostly to other non-management responsibilities and increased spans of control) as the number one reason they don't more consistently practice the basics of management."

In my executive leadership coaching practice, one of the first things I do with clients is have them examine how they spend their time. I'm still trying to figure out how to help my clients get more than 24 hours in a day, but so far I've been unsuccessful! The problem is that economic challenges of recent years, downsizing, increased responsibilities and a

THE DILEMMA OF "UNDER-MANAGING" AND TIME

tight labor market create a legitimate sense of fear that everyone's jobs are at risk. A tsunami of factors has made the jobs of managers and leaders even more complex and difficult.

In the time analysis my clients do, I use this matrix from the work of Stephen Covey in his book *First Things First.*[20]

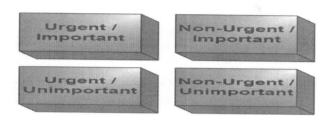

Some brief highlights of this model:

Urgent/Important: These are key things you have responsibility for (and probably others are dependent on you for) that have near-term time sensitivity. Beware that they can feed your "urgency addiction" that is fueled by adrenaline.

Urgent/Unimportant: These are meetings, communications and events that are important to others but perhaps less important for you in terms of the goals you are responsible for. We often attend meetings or read unimportant email out of habit or a sense of duty without really considering the cost/benefit use of our time.

Non-Urgent/Unimportant: Never mind. Covey says that reasonably productive leaders spend very little time here.

Non-Urgent/Important: This is the most important of the four quadrants, where the rubber hits the road in terms of making your mark as a leader. Here are the critical things that occur in this quadrant:

- Preparing for meetings, presentations and customers
- Planning for initiatives, budgeting, performance reviews and feedback, implementing new processes

- Prevention of mistakes by attention to process and an investment in training
- Relationship building, getting to know and build trust with key constituents inside and outside of your organization
- Empowering your team, working to clarify boundaries, expectations, review cycles and performance metrics

A time analysis is not difficult, but making the tough choices to get more out of your time is challenging. You must first identify what you need to stop doing. (See the chapter in this section "To Enhance Productivity, Stop Doing Something!") One of the worst challenges for leaders is failing to make time for reflection (meditation) so they can learn from what they are experiencing (wisdom). I have tremendous empathy for leaders in this incredibly fast-paced world. I am not advocating daily meditation at work, although I certainly believe it wouldn't hurt anything, but here are a couple key things I would like you to consider to better engage your staff and provide more satisfaction for you:

1. Set aside time on Thursday afternoon to plan for the following week. Don't do it on Friday, or on Sunday night and certainly not on Monday morning. By setting aside at least 30 minutes to contemplate the key things that are on the calendar for the following week, you have time on Friday to begin planning meetings and work to make them happen. Jealously guard this time on Thursday and make time Friday to begin the follow-ups you have identified.

2. As a leader, your time is a very precious commodity. Make a ruthless analysis of all the meetings you attend and all the email you sort through. Can you ask for notes from the meetings you can't attend or can you delegate someone to go for you? If you fail to read someone's weekly report three weeks in a row, chances are you can just skip it. If you subscribe to newsletters you once thought would be fun to read in your spare time but don't ever get

THE DILEMMA OF "UNDER-MANAGING" AND TIME

around to them, unsubscribe now.

That's all you may have time for in the short run. If you can put some energy into planning and delegating, you will feel more highly engaged and your team will reflect that, making the work more productive and fulfilling for everyone involved.

Ask yourself:

- What can I do to prevent the costs of under-management and better engage my team?

- How can I arrange my time to put first things first? What tasks can I delegate to ensure I concentrate on urgent and important things?

- Where in my Thursday schedule can I fit 30 minutes dedicated to planning for the following week?

MAKE TIME FOR YOURSELF BY BECOMING MORE EFFICIENT

Isn't it amazing how much stuff we get done before vacation?
—Zig ZIGLAR

IT IS IMPORTANT FOR LEADERS to get out of town—or at least out of the office—so they can recharge and so their team members can learn to step up in their absence. It's amazing how much productivity you demonstrate when getting ready to leave for vacation. You answer email, delegate things you'd been meaning to deal with and make a flurry of follow-up calls. Often the pressure of leaving can really elevate your decision making and energy. You may even get a warm feeling when you walk out the door and look at the order on your desk and review the lengthy check list of things you completed.

The Disappearing Vacation

But the trend in the United States is toward less time away from the office. According to a 2012 survey conducted by The Conference Board, Inc., a global business and research association based in New York City, the statistics are alarming:

- Forty percent of American workers had no plans to take a vacation over the next six months, the lowest percentage recorded by the group in 28 years.
- Fifty-seven percent of American workers had unused vacation time, and in a typical year, that amounts to 175 million vacation days not taken.
- Since 1970, Americans on average work an additional 568 hours per year, about another 10 hours per week.

- Twenty-three percent of American workers in the private sector do not get any paid vacation time.
- The average vacation duration has been reduced from seven to four days—by choice. (This choice is motivated by fear. Staffs are thin so there is no back-up and employees fear that if something goes wrong in their absence, they will lose their jobs.)

If you've done business in Europe, you're aware that many companies close or run with minimal staff during the month of August, when the majority of employees go on vacation. I had a three-year assignment in Germany, and my clients there scoffed at the idea of a one-week vacation. They claimed you needed three weeks to have a real vacation—one week to unwind, one week to really relax and one week for reentry. My English peers in my last corporate role also jealously guarded their vacation time, and those businesses seemed to hum right along despite such liberal vacation practices.

Why does failing to take time away from work seem to be such an American malady? By letting technology run amok, American society has created an artificial reality where busyness is now equated with our value to an organization. We can't seem to escape the email, texts, calls and meetings. Such communications cross continents and time zones, complicating matters even more. What it says to us is that if we are busy, we must be important, and if we are important, we must be on call 24/7.

Reasons to Take Time Away

The executives I have come to admire seem to be the most responsive but also the most in demand. They manage busyness rather than let themselves be controlled by it. These people find ways to take vacations so they can enjoy their families, indulge in their passions and recharge their batteries. I tell my executive clients that because of the stress they are exposed to, by the end of every quarter they should have their vacation time planned for the following quarter, even if it's only an extended weekend. Having a break to look forward to is always a positive thing.

A couple of years ago I came across an interesting article in the *Fast Company* newsletter by Patty Azzarello (June 26, 2012) titled, "Think You Can't Take a Vacation? The Sound Business Reasons You Really Should." Some of the reasons she gave that the business is better off without you for a while include:

1. It shows you are a competent leader. If you can plan, delegate and free up time for yourself and not leave a train wreck while you're away, it is a positive reflection on your leadership skills.

2. Nobody is impressed that you haven't taken a vacation in years. The old saying is that all work and no play makes Jack or Jill a dull person. People do not respect or admire someone who can't get away.

3. You will motivate your team. They will appreciate your example of allowing yourself to have a life as long as you don't insist on checking in and sending them emails while you're away.

4. Your team can be more productive. You may not like to hear it, but the absence of all the stuff that you normally throw at them gives your team a chance to catch up on their own work.

5. When you're unreachable, your team has opportunities to develop and grow. They'll have to stretch themselves, learn and take some risks. Just don't undo or overrule all they have done when you get back.

6. You will be more productive. When you have a chance to reflect and mull over some tough issues without day-to-day pressures, you may be surprised at the insights that present themselves.

7. It may help you prioritize better. In the busyness that is our world, priorities are overwhelmed by the adrenaline rush of constant action. Being away should help your perspective.

8. You and your company benefit. People who indulge in interests outside work tend to deal better with pressures and disappointments in the workplace.

Focusing on Efficiency and Effectiveness

Sometimes people tell me they hesitate to take time off because when they return from an absence, things have piled up so much that being away just isn't worth it. But if you focus on efficiency and effectiveness year-round, you can control the deluge of "stuff" coming at you— email, check-ins with the boss and team, new meetings, employee needs and more.

The pre-vacation efficiency that you exercise is a product of the time pressure of your departure. So at other times, you need a model, and David Allen, a personal productivity guru whose work I have followed for years, has a great model for dealing with all the "stuff" (see *Getting Things Done: The Art of Stress-Free Productivity*, Viking, 2001, New York, New York, page 139).

Using Allen's simple model will help you enhance your efficiency and effectiveness and make you more comfortable about taking time away from the office.

- For anything that crosses your desk, quickly determine what is FYI and what needs action.
- If something needs no immediate action, throw it away, put it on your to-do list or file it. And keep your filing system simple so anyone would be able to decipher it if you got hit by a bus.
- Move emails or documents pertaining to current projects into appropriate files or electronic folders.

- If something can be taken care of in two minutes or less, do it immediately and be done. Keep your responses brief.
- If something is more complicated, defer it or delegate it. Fine tune your systems for keeping track of things and always be willing to improve and enhance as you go.

As Peter Drucker says in *The Effective Executive*, "Efficiency is doing things right; effectiveness is doing the right things." When you're constantly bombarded with information, it can feel like you're drinking from a fire hose. To enhance efficiency and effectiveness, you need to focus on priorities. What really needs to be done in the next 90 days? Write these things down in large print and hang the list on a wall of your office. Then, with those goals as your guideline, purge all the stuff that's accumulated in your office that isn't relevant. Get rid of all the magazines and reports you intended to read but haven't. Go through all the files and folders that have piled up and be ruthless about getting rid of things and clearing your path to higher levels of effectiveness. Focus is the key to productivity! Here are some tips to keep in mind:

- Give yourself a few uninterrupted hours to accomplish a purge. Come in early or stay late or even do it on a weekend.
- Bring in several trash receptacles.
- Get someone to help you toss stuff or put post-its on the stuff you need to file or delegate.
- If this works well for you—and it should—use it as a model for the whole team to do at least twice a year.

Ask yourself:
- Do I think I'm too busy or important to take a vacation?
- Could I be stifling the development of my team?
- Can I find ways to improve my everyday efficiency and effectiveness so it's easier to let go and take time off?

DON'T WAIT UNTIL SPRING—DO A CLEAN SWEEP ANYTIME

Out of clutter, find simplicity. From discord, find harmony. In the middle of difficulty lies opportunity.
— Albert Einstein

KEEPING THINGS ORGANIZED is critical to your success. If you are a gardener, you trim trees to help them grow, weed around plants to help them thrive and prune bushes to allow them to flourish. Do the same to your office, workspace or home to be more efficient and save time looking for things that should be at hand.

In Japanese culture, the time before the New Year is used to clean, declutter, finish pending projects and get organized. It is referred to as "*kure*." Over the years, I have helped several clients "put their houses in order," usually on a Saturday morning. One client inherited an unbelievable mess as the business manager of a school district and it took us more than one day. We quit on the first day because we had filled all the dumpsters.

I would like to suggest the following five things for your office purge:

1. Set aside a day for getting organized. If you have some downtime during the holidays, plan it for then. Give yourself at least four hours to purge, file and reorganize.

2. If you are a leader, make housecleaning an event. It can get really boring to do by yourself and if you make it a group event:

   • Have some food and music,

113

- Bring in some extra trash receptacles/recycling containers,
- Have someone else be your accountability partner and help you sort through your "stuff," and
- Have extra folders and expandable files readily available.

3. Make lists/piles of stuff for filing or storage. Try to touch things only twice!

4. Set ground rules about various types of information:

   - If it was something you intended to read but it's more than six months old, toss it!
   - If it's material in a file about a project you intended to work on but haven't touched in six months, is it still a viable area of focus? If not, toss it!
   - If it's material someone else may need, prepare it to send to them.
   - If your office gets nice and tidy but your staff gets all your stuff, you are not doing this right.

5. When you are done, or the time expires (because you are too indecisive, nostalgic or addicted to clutter), ask yourself or sit with your team and have everyone consider how often purge days are needed and how much more productive you'll feel when you've accomplished the task.

I wish you the very best for your office purge. While you are filled with the joy of accomplishment for your efforts, also consider:

Clothes Closet Purge: Go through the clothes in your closets. Do you need seven hats or six pairs of gloves? Have you worn that item in the last two years? Do you think you will ever wear it again? If not, donate it! Your gently worn garments may be a real blessing to someone else.

Holiday Decorations/Ornaments Purge: I realize some of these have sentimental value, but consider the storage space you can save. Of course, the best time to do this is before or after the holidays, when everything is out anyway.

Car Purge: Many of us use our cars all the time. Some of us practically live in them! Clear out the trunk except for things you need for emergencies. Clean out the glove compartment and other storage spaces in the doors, midsection and back seat. Give the inside a good clean.

I realize these suggestions will not rise to the level of "Boy, that sounds like real fun," but each is important. And like the office purge, each of them is better done with others. Get some help to make it easier.

Ask yourself:

- What will I do to reduce my clutter in the coming year?

- Is there a project I had neglected that I am now reenergized to pursue?

- What tricks or ideas did I learn from my coworkers that are insightful and I will use going forward?

COMMUNICATION

INTRO: COMMUNICATING FOR IMPACT AND INFLUENCE

IN THE CONTEXT OF LEADERSHIP, I define communication as the process of being heard as well as hearing others. When one person has a message that he or she is sending to another individual or a group, a communication "vibration" occurs between the parties. Whether or not there is congruency in what the sender intended and what the receiver received is dependent on a wide set of variables. This section will explore elements that facilitate effective communication and some obvious barriers that prevent it.

Sender / Receiver Communications

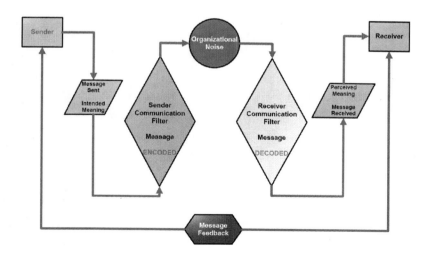

This chart conveys the challenges of communicating effectively. Messages or topics can be complicated. Time pressures may limit dialogue in the exchange of meaningful information. Poorly run meetings can choke off valuable debate or veer into tangents that scuttle meaningful dialogue. Poor communication also reflects the filters that both senders and receivers bring to the interchange. These filters reflect different experiences, education, motivations, incentives and pressures. They are not consciously used to reduce clarity but they reflect the complexity of the task.

I have first-hand experience as an executive as well as a coach in trying to communicate with multiple cultures at the same time, with all the complexity that language differences add. One area everyone involved in any dialogue needs to keep in mind is their role in the exchange of information. Different roles to consider include:

- **A subject matter expert:** Someone whose background and experience is valuable in gaining the best possible options and insights for the question or issue at hand
- **An observer:** Someone just trying to get up to speed on the status or purpose of an initiative
- **A facilitator:** Someone whose role is like a catalyst, meant to move the meeting and dialogue along but usually in a neutral role
- **A leader:** The person who is trying to harness the opinions of others toward some organizational purpose or goal

When you consider the interactions that you have with individuals or with a group, it can be valuable to ensure you understand the scope and limits of your role.

Communication Opportunities

We communicate in a variety of ways, including written documents, email, instant messages, phone calls, voicemail, presentations and meeting participation. In addition to these, face-to-face communications exchange information, provide performance feedback, sell your vision or purpose, negotiate and help resolve conflicts. I would argue that face-to-face communications are the most effective way we influence others. As a manager or leader, you have to purposefully influence others to promote your solutions, suggestions and the benefits of your expertise.

The two key communication skills for face-to-face communications are speaking and listening. Key elements of both can enhance your understanding of how to get the very best out of your communications. In some regard, it's amazing how inextricably linked speaking and listening are. Your speaking skills are critical for both expressing your message and for using questions and an interrogatory style to help you respond in a manner that enhances mutual understanding, demonstrates empathy for another's needs and perspectives, ensures you are heard and facilitates progress toward solutions that are valued.

We listen on three levels:

1. **Level 1:** Listening to hear the words and translate them into useful pieces of information.

2. **Level 2:** Listening for the thoughts being expressed with the purpose of planning your response or next question. This often results in shortchanging the speaker's message because we are hard at work preparing what we wish to say.

3. **Level 3:** Engaging in active listening that helps us to fully focus on the person who is speaking, their thoughts, feelings and what's unspoken.

Becoming adept at Level 3 listening requires that, as Stephen Covey says, "Seek first to understand and then to be understood." You must use your interaction to first of all inquire about the set of facts that the person you are speaking with has used for the foundation of their argument or perspective. We want to inquire, not interrogate, to determine the who, what, why, where, when and how of any situation. Granted, there may be agreement on many of these points, but on any that are uncertain or when there is a risk of different facts or a difference of opinion, it is critical that you drill down to find common understanding.

With those facts in mind, it is time to ask follow-up questions to allow the other person to elaborate about their perspective or suggestion. You are not trying to put them on the stand or grill them, but you do want to find ways to enhance understanding of the facts at hand. For instance, here are some examples of the lead into good follow-up questions:

- "For example?"
- "Specifically?"
- "Tell me more."
- "Why do you say that?"

It is important that you are as patient as possible in trying to create this additional level of clarity and awareness for everyone who is involved in the conversation, even if it's just the two of you. Be careful not to put the other person on the defensive, but every additional piece of clarity that is gained should help the quality of the possible outcomes.

After this it is usually effective to summarize/play back what you have heard to allow for any more back and forth to gain additional clarity. For instance:

- "Let me be sure I understand your position . . ."
- "If I understand you correctly . . . "
- "So what you are saying/suggesting is . . . "

At this point, your conversation should have encouraged a successful back and forth about the facts of the situation, the needs of each party and possibly several key options or solutions. We often avoid this interrogatory process because we do not want to make the other person feel as if we are grilling them, but asking questions makes common understanding of the issues at hand easier to achieve.

If you want to enhance the effectiveness of your management and leadership skills, you must become more aware of the vocal and visual cues you get in your interactions with others. Your ability to concentrate on not only the words but also the thoughts and feelings that are conveyed in vocal and visual cues will enhance your understanding and effectiveness by several degrees.

Many people over-rely on email communications. Instant messaging and text messaging are subsets of email but they have one common trait: They are only a written reflection of the communication vibration; they are just the words themselves. If you track how much of your communication is done via email, you may realize that you are foregoing 90 percent of the impact of making an effective communication a reality. If you are trying to communicate information using only these tools, you are missing an opportunity to influence others.

Electronic communication conveys 10 percent of the possible communication impact. When we speak with somebody on the phone, we get about 45 percent of the communication impact because we are adding tone, pace, and volume to our understanding. It is only when we can observe the other person's body language, their level of arousal, approach or dominance that we can truly get 100 percent of the communication vibration. (And even then, you can be mistaken!) The efficiency of exchanging information is much greater with electronic tools like email and text messaging, but the effectiveness of the communication is obviously better in person. Today's standard of communicating globally argues for greater use of technologies like Skype or video conferencing to enhance communications.

Listening techniques and greater attention to all these elements of communication won't solve all the issues that come up in your organization. Difficult people, incomplete information, a politicized dynamic regarding the issue at hand and a host of organizational uncertainties create legitimate anxieties. I have never met an argumentative or unpleasant individual who described himself as "difficult." They just believe they have a different point of view and a different way of expressing it than you might. Not all of these individuals are Machiavellians who believe that the end justifies the means, but they often can make interactions unpleasant and ineffective. They may take an aggressive stance and try to overpower or bully others into reaching agreements. This is not a way to develop effective long-term relationships in an organization.

Communicating to Solve Problems

This discussion about communicating for impact and influence is based on the exchange of ideas among professionals for the purposes of making business decisions to drive toward organizational goals. The most effective way to communicate is in person, but since that is not always cost-effective, many decisions are made via conference calls or video-conferences. Keeping these communication ideas in mind should help move any discussion forward effectively, unless a common issue of group dynamics is allowed to disrupt a productive problem-solving discussion. A simple model for the flow of a problem-solving dialogue is as follows:

What's up: Simply state what is going on and encourage questions to confirm understanding.

What's so: Test thinking to agree on the facts at hand and for any updates on information that moves the discussion forward.

What's possible: Brainstorm possible solutions to consider. It is important to generate a variety of options so if whatever option is chosen fails to work, you've already considered other avenues to pursue.

Let's go: Confirm the action plan and delegate responsibilities.

My experience with many organizations is that they are simply impatient and will often commit to one of the earlier options for action that is raised. They fail to consider alternatives or spend too little time on the current facts. One critical factor in communications is that everyone is challenged for time to plan and prepare for important meetings. But such preparations yield greater results and show much greater respect for the people in attendance. A good meeting leader will also ensure that the notes of the meeting, including all decisions made and who's responsible for action items, will be clearly articulated and disseminated as quickly as possible. The stakes are high when you're communicating about programs, policies or organizational goals and direction.

This introduction to communications is primarily geared toward enhancing the level of credibility that you create for yourself within your organization. By embracing some of these ideas, you can influence how you are perceived. If people see you as assertive and consistent in the verbal, vocal and visual aspects of the communication vibration you create, they will be drawn to working with you. People admire honest and competent individuals with whom they can interact and want to do business with people they like and trust. Good communication skills go a long way toward creating the trust that is critical in any organization.

As a leader, you have an obligation to ensure that those you lead or try to influence understand what you are saying and why you are saying it, and to communicate effectively you must understand how others perceive your message. If your awareness is diminished, your communication may be more accidental, putting at risk your credibility and your ability to lead or influence. You can enhance your chances of success through preparation and practicing what you intend to say and why.

The newest computer can merely compound, at speed,
the oldest problem in the relations between human beings,
and in the end the communicator will be confronted
with the old problem of what to say and how to say it.
—EDWARD R. MURROW

Ten Ways to Listen Better
and Be Fully Present

*There is a difference between listening and
waiting for your turn to speak.*
—Simon Sinek

Tuesdays with Morrie is a book by Mitch Albom that came out in 1997 and topped the bestsellers list for nonfiction and was also made into a movie. It is about Morrie Schwartz, a former Brandeis University sociology professor who contracted ALS, commonly known as Lou Gehrig's disease, and the relationship Albom rekindled with him after seeing a "Nightline" television news report about how Morrie was dealing with this crippling and fatal condition. I thought about it recently when I encountered a couple of situations, both personal and professional, where I was challenged to be a good listener.

Albom came to visit Morrie on Tuesdays just to reconnect with his former teacher, whom he had not spoken with since graduating 16 years earlier. Here's what Albom had to say about a key thing that resonated with him about this connection:

> "I came to love the way Morrie lit up when I entered the room. He did this for many people, I know, but it was his special talent to make each visitor feel that the smile was unique.
>
> "AHHHH, it's my buddy," he would say when he saw me, in that foggy, high-pitched voice. And it didn't stop with the greeting. When Morrie was with you, he was really with you. He looked you straight in the eye, and he listened as if you were the only person in the world. How much better would people get along if their first encounter each day were like this— instead of a grumble from a waitress or a bus driver or a boss?

127

"I believe in being fully present," Morrie said. "That means you should be with the person you're with. When I'm talking to you now, Mitch, I try to keep focused only on what is going on between us. I am not thinking about something we said last week. I am not thinking about what's coming up this Friday. I am not thinking about doing another Koppel show or about what medications I'm taking. I am talking to you. I am thinking about you."

I remembered how he used to teach this idea on the Group Process class back at Brandeis. I had scoffed back then, thinking this was hardly a lesson plan for a university course. Learning to pay attention? How important could that be? I now know that it is more important than almost everything they taught us in college."[21]

This simple notion of being fully present is often overwhelmed by the cacophony of noise and the invited avalanche of bright shiny objects that pop up on our smartphones, computers, tablets and TVs that are on everywhere, all the time. Some of this noise can be useful and productive when we can sort out the important from the trivial, but that can be hard to do. Lost in this tsunami of stimulation is the ability to be at peace long enough to have a meaningful conversation and demonstrate our interest in another's worldview or needs.

Marshall Goldsmith, author and executive leadership coach, spoke to this very point in his blog "The Skill that Separates" (June 16, 2014):

"And listening requires the discipline to concentrate. So I've developed a simple exercise to test my clients' listening skills. Close your eyes. Count slowly to 50 with one simple goal: You can't let another thought intrude into your mind. You must concentrate on maintaining the count.

Sounds simple, but incredibly, more than half of my clients can't do it. Somewhere around 20 or 30, nagging thoughts invade their brains. They think about a problem at work, or their kids, or how much they ate for dinner the night before. This may sound like a concentration test, but it's really a listening exercise. After all, if you can't listen to yourself (someone you presumably like) as you count to 50, how will you ever be able to listen to another person?

Like any exercise, this drill both exposes a weakness and helps us get stronger. If I ask you to touch your toes and you can't, we've revealed that your muscles are tight. But if you practice each day, eventually you'll become more limber."[22]

I do not have a magic prescription for creating a "fully present" connection, but I do have some suggestions about how you can engage in more productive business and personal conversations. Listening, really listening, with our whole being, is a skill and one of the most important compliments we can give another human being.

My Top Ten Rules for Effective Listening

1. Stop talking! It is difficult to listen and speak at the same time.

2. Put the other person at ease. Give them space and time to speak. How you look at them and how you stand or sit make a huge difference. Relax, and let them relax as well.

3. Show the other person that you want to hear them. Look at them. Nod when you agree. Ask them to explain if you don't understand. Listen to understand them and their words, rather than just wait for your turn to respond.

4. Remove distractions. Good listening means being willing to ignore the phone, close a door or stop reading your mail. Give

others your full attention, and let them know they are getting your full attention.

5. Empathize with the other person, especially if they are telling you something painful or something you intensely disagree with. Take a moment to stand in their shoes, to look at the situation from their point of view. Empathy is highly correlated to executive success.

6. Be patient. Some people take longer to find the right word, to make a point or clarify an issue. Give the speaker time to get it all out before you jump in with your reply. Never finish someone else's statements for them. If you have a time constraint, tell the other person up front and be willing to provide a specific time for a follow-up conversation later.

7. Watch your own emotions. If what someone says creates an emotional response in you, be extra vigilant to listen carefully, with attention to the intent and full meaning of their words. When we are angry, frightened or upset, we often miss critical parts of what is being said to us.

8. Be slow to disagree, criticize or argue. Even if you disagree, let them have their point of view. If you respond in a way that makes the other person defensive, even if you win the argument, you may lose something far more valuable, like an effective working relationship.

9. Ask lots of questions. Encourage others to clarify, say more, give an example or explain further. It will help them speak more precisely and it will help you hear and understand them more accurately.

10. Stop talking! This is both the first and the last point, because all other points depend on it. Nature gave us two ears and only one tongue, which is a gentle hint that we should listen twice as much as we talk.

Ask yourself:

- Which three of these rules would have the greatest impact on improving my listening? Focus on them for the next month and see what happens.

- How long can I concentrate on just one thing, like counting to 50, that reflects my ability to focus?

THE LISTENING CHALLENGE

One of the best ways to persuade others is
with your ears—by listening to them.
—DEAN RUSK

EARLY IN MY COACHING CAREER, I worked two years for a man named Frank who had established a vibrant coaching practice. He was an excellent salesman and exuded an air of executive gravitas that was fitting with his experience—and his shock of silver hair. He told me a story of a sales call he made, based on a referral, to a senior executive of a major Chicago-based company. The fellow's assistant made it clear that he could spare only 30 minutes, and although Frank liked closer to an hour to connect with a prospective client, he took what he could get.

The executive came out from behind his desk in his elegant office and sat face to face with Frank in a small sitting area. He gave Frank his rapt attention and asked several insightful questions along the way. At the 25-minute mark, his assistant knocked and reminded him he needed to leave in five minutes. Frank wrapped up his pitch and, like any good salesman, asked for the order. The executive very politely and firmly explained why Frank's services were not a fit for his company and brought the meeting to a close. Frank asked where he was off to, and the executive said he was giving an important presentation to a major Chicago civic group—in one hour!

Frank told me this story because it was an excellent example of someone demonstrating active listening with a complete focus on the person speaking. Frank described it as the most impressive "no" he ever got. It would have been understandable if this fellow had been impatient, distracted or disinterested. It's a rare person who can provide such a level of focus, but the most successful people have this ability to show interest, ask questions and listen to the answers without distraction. I have a friend who was a classmate of Hillary Clinton's in grade school and high school. Although she is a die-hard Republican, she has said that Bill Clinton has this unique skill—he listens like you are the only person in the room—often among a throng of others.

In coaching clients, I use an online assessment that provides insight about listening styles. It breaks the listening process into two areas—a focus on feelings and a focus on information.

Feeling Orientation

- Appreciative Listening: To relax and enjoy the listening experience
- Empathic Listening: To support and understand the emotions of others

Information Orientation

- Discerning Listening: To gather complete and accurate information
- Comprehensive Listening: To organize information and understand the meaning of the message
- Evaluative Listening: To critique information and make a decision

In my work with clients, I always stress how important the skill of listening is to their effectiveness as leaders. Although all five of these listening elements are important, knowing when to stress one over another reflects the wisdom of experience.

- If someone is "unloading" about a situation that did not go as planned, go heavy on the empathy until you know it's time to help them rethink the issue.

- When someone seems to be missing the bigger picture or discounting certain variables, drill down more on comprehensive listening to better understand and provide better guidance.
- One of the biggest concerns I hear is how some leaders jump into evaluative listening too early. Sometimes others want us to be a sounding board so they can develop their own answers.

Listening is a complex process. Two key traits of the best listeners are the patience to listen deeply and completely and the ability to project a true connection with others. Very few people have those unique skills.

Ask yourself:

- Can I really focus on others, ask good, insightful questions and make them feel like they are the most important people to me while we chat?

- Will I try to conquer the "Count to 50" exercise until I can do it consistently?

- Can I refrain from evaluating what I have heard long enough to be sure if the speaker wants an answer or just for me to listen?

FOUR REASONS TO USE SILENCE TO COMMUNICATE MORE POWERFULLY

The more a man speaks, the less he is understood.
—ABRAHAM LINCOLN

THE OTHER DAY I RAN INTO a fellow who is the reluctant president of a board I am on. He's an accomplished individual but quiet and reserved by nature. I don't think he enjoys his leadership role, but I used this chance encounter to ask again about a pending issue before the board. I calmly stated my position, asking for time for us to consider this thorny issue. He did not respond, and the "deer in the headlights" look on his face made me want to drop the subject and move on with my day. But instead, I maintained a neutral look on my face and just calmly waited for his response in silence. After this awkward silence, he agreed to call me that evening and he did.

In communicating, it's been shown that words account for 10 percent of what's expressed; vocal tone and pace, 35 percent; and nonverbal communication, 55 percent. Silence is a critical aspect of nonverbal communication. It is vastly underutilized but it's a powerful element of communicating when used purposefully. Here are four reasons that you should consider for using silence to everyone's advantage in communications.

Silence allows you to think, breathe, listen and hold the attention of the listener.

Muhammad Ali, who usually was expert with words, said, "Silence is golden when you can't think of a good answer." When it's your turn to speak, pausing before you respond gives you some time to gather your thoughts, choose your words and heighten the expectation of others about what you may say. I'm not suggesting you delay to build suspense, but pausing silently reflects a deeper, more thoughtful response.

I am reminded of asking my father questions at the dinner table; we had some interesting dialogues growing up. When my brother was about six, he declared that he knew a million facts. My father paused and asked him if he knew about some random topic. My brother paused, considered my father's question and meekly responded, "Well, that's not one of them!" and proceeded to quietly eat his dinner. I thought my parents were going to convulse with laughter, but it is a perfect example of this effect.

Silence allows others to invest in your ideas.

When you pause before responding to a direct question or after you have posed a question to the group or another team member, you allow others to process what you have said and consider their response. It gives everyone time to step back and reflect on how what's been said affects them, their team and the organization. It also projects a confidence on your part that you refuse to be rushed by circumstances. Leonardo da Vinci said, "Nothing strengthens authority so much as silence."

Silence always seems longer than it is.

In today's world of instantaneous communication, we're consistently bombarded with texts, email and information that flows from a constant connection to the Internet. It's a tsunami of distractions and impulses that we allow to overwhelm us. So the idea of literally stopping that rush and pausing, even for effect, is becoming even more foreign to us. But if you recognize that someone you respect seems to be able to use this tool effectively, count how long they wait before they respond and you'll see that it is probably 15 seconds or less. Fifteen seconds doesn't seem like a very long time, but in today's world of lightning fast connections, it may seem longer.

Your silence allows others to express themselves.

In my interaction with my fellow board member, I went through the mental process of telling myself not to respond and to wait for his reaction. Often when you see someone hesitating or uncomfortable, you will feel compelled to rush in to "rescue them." This is a noble sentiment, but you lose the opportunity to encourage them to state their case. You should not purposely try to inflict any additional angst on their part, but you should give them the time and space to compose their response to you.

While you wait, you need to ensure that you maintain a neutral to positive nonverbal affect in your facial expressions. Do not glare, raise your eyebrows or appear too eager for the response.

Ask yourself:

- Do I have the patience and confidence to pause for effect before responding?

- Have I observed others who seem to use silence effectively? Am I willing to time how long they are silent before responding to get a sense of how short a time it takes to be more effective?

- Can I avoid trying to rescue someone during an awkward pause to allow them time to gather themselves for their response?

THREE TYPES OF SILENT MESSAGES THAT SPEAK LOUDLY

The most important thing in communication is hearing what isn't said.
—PETER DRUCKER

I took some out-of-town guests to see a show at Second City. Second City has had a remarkable influence on comedy since it began in the 1950s. The number of "Saturday Night Live" alumni who hail from Second City is substantial. I always enjoy the late show on the weekend because after the regular show, the troupe comes out to do live improvisation and the audience can call out the topics. It's wildly inventive and a joy to see the performers strut their stuff.

During this most recent visit, one of the members of the troupe walked into the audience, grabbed my hand and pulled me on stage for five minutes that both frightened and delighted me. Not one word was spoken between the female actor and me as we fed each other pudding and then shared a couple beers—all imaginary of course. I had fun with it, and the audience gave me a nice hand when I sat down.

As I described this adventure to a friend the other night, it made me reflect on the fact that all the behavior was nonverbal. No words were spoken but we engaged in light-hearted interaction. This made me consider the critical importance of not only nonverbal communication but the nonverbal cues that we both give and interpret in our regular business and personal interactions.

Knowing the three broad areas of these cues can provide some insight about how you react and how you might be able to take advantage of these insights to make your communication more effective. Please be aware that there is nothing absolute about any of these observations; the context of the situation and the quality of the relationship among those interacting can also influence silent messages that are conveyed. Just being aware of nonverbal cues will help you recognize and use them to reduce the unintended consequences of their potential impact.

Approach/Avoidance

We approach or move toward those things that we like or are attracted to. We tend to pull back, even recoil, from those things that are unpleasant or that we would rather avoid. We may not think along these lines when it comes to ideas or the business associates who are communicating those ideas, but our nonverbal behavior projects these types of reactions. Here are several behavioral cues that display this nonverbal reality:

Proximity: We tend to sit or stand closer to those we like or are drawn to.

Touching: We may reach out to touch an elbow or put a hand on someone's shoulder when we're making a point, but we rarely do that to those we may be less favorably inclined toward.

Attentiveness: If someone whom we admire or respect is speaking, we tend to shut out distractions more easily and maintain focus. Even if we don't care for the individual, we will be more attentive if the subject interests us.

Handshakes: A firm, friendly handshake, especially coupled with good eye contact, says a lot when we greet someone or say goodbye. A soft or wimpy handshake may be a style issue, and a crushing grip may project aggressiveness.

Questions: We will tend to ask more questions on topics we are drawn to, unless we choose to pepper the speaker in an aggressive or accusatory manner with a volume of questions.

Seating Angle: We tend to lean into a speaker when we are interested in or attracted to them or the topic. We tend to pull back and away from those people or topics that have the opposite effect. Caution: some people pull back momentarily to simply ponder a situation; they will probably lean back in when they hear something on a topic that appeals to them.

Arousal/Non-Arousal

We get excited about ideas and the people we are interacting with when they interest us. We tend to withdraw or get distracted when we are not. Here are several behavioral cues that display this nonverbal reality:

Facial Expressiveness: Our facial expressions denote interest, joy or fascination with raised eyebrows, smiles and nodding in agreement. When we dislike a speaker or their ideas, you'll see frowns, headshaking or even puzzled looks.

Rate of Speech: When we're excited about an idea, we tend to speak more quickly and in a more animated fashion. The opposite of this is not always dislike of an idea; some folks purposely slow down the rate of speech to add emphasis.

Volume: Our enthusiasm or support for an idea will oftentimes lead to speaking in increased volumes. Short, curt responses at low volumes can show the opposite.

Open vs. Closed Gestures: Open gestures such as open palms or active gesticulating can denote a positive take on an idea; whereas, crossed arms and pulling back in the chair can often denote a lack of interest or hostility to an idea.

Eye Contact: Consistent eye contact with a speaker shows that you are interested and drinking in what they have to say. Rolling or averting the eyes, shows the opposite effect. Glaring at someone with an intense stare and other elements of facial expression can reflect concern or disbelief.

Dominance/Submissiveness

In some regards, this category reflects gender differences and biases that may exist. The demonstration of dominance or submissiveness is often probably not purposely projected, but these not-so-subtle cues do convey significant meaning. Here are several behavioral cues that display this nonverbal reality:

Relaxed Posture: If you sit in a very symmetrical manner with your arms and legs straight, you may project an image of the kid who is called to the principal's office. If you cross your legs or sit more asymmetrically in a chair, that relaxed posture can project a level of confidence and control.

Comfortable/Tense: It's pretty normal to be tense in a new situation with new people. That natural apprehensiveness keeps you on your "emotional toes" until you reach a level of comfort with the people or situation you're involved with. There are times when you'll want to coach yourself to not appear tense.

Sit/Stand: This cue relates to the symmetry of a situation. Standing over somebody who is sitting is referred to as a "power distance." If both people are either standing or sitting, that power distance can be mitigated. Walking in and sitting down in someone's office tends to "level the playing field."

Respect for Personal Space: The idea of personal space is the amount of distance that people are comfortable with in interacting with others. The differences in the personal definition of this span gender, cultural and international factors. I have one good friend whose definition of personal space seems to be about four inches. Trust and familiarity will give you better insights into this issue over time.

These cues can help you develop the critical nonverbal element of the communication vibration you project to others. Use it to help diagnose what bothers you and as a tool to improve your impact on others.

Ask yourself:

- Are there a couple of nonverbal responses that convey silent messages that I did not intend recently? How could I have adjusted my responses to be more effective or reduce any unintended negatives?

- "How can I adjust my silent messages" to purposely demonstrate more support for ideas or a person in meetings?

- What is one nonverbal behavior that I can more purposefully engage in to show my influence in a positive manner?

Adapted from Albert Mehrabian, *Silent Messages: Implicit Communication of Emotions and Attitudes.* (Belmont, CA: Wadsworth Publishing, 1981).

USING I-LANGUAGE ASSERTIVENESS IN YOUR INTERACTIONS

*Courage is contagious. When a brave man takes a stand,
the spines of others are often stiffened.*
—BILLY GRAHAM

MARSHALL GOLDSMITH IS perhaps the preeminent executive coach in America. A key part of his Stakeholder Centered Coaching model, which I now use, requires the client to identify one key goal that could have the greatest potential impact on that executive's performance and to solicit monthly feedback on progress toward its accomplishment. This model has proven to be incredibly effective in changing behavior.

A key element of the model requires the client to ask stakeholders if they are willing to participate in the process. The first thing the model requires is that a stakeholder is willing to let go of the past and not allow it to shade perceptions going forward. Although this makes perfect sense, in practice it is often not easy to do. It requires a leap of faith on the part of the stakeholder to give the executive the benefit of the doubt about his or her ability to change or shape his or her behavior for the better. Sometimes that is a tall order if the prior behavior had been particularly difficult or damaging. It's not really asking for forgiveness, and that's fortunate, given how difficult that can be to find. In Randy Pausch's book, *The Last Lecture*,[23] I found this interesting passage:

"Moravian missionaries searched for a word for forgiveness in the Eskimo language. That's when they discovered 'issumagijoujung-nainermik,' a 24-letter tongue-twister, which literally means 'not being able to think about it anymore.' Genuine forgiveness is about moving on and refusing to think any more about what happened."

I am not going to explore the complex and challenging topic of forgiveness other than to share this wonderful quote from Mahatma Gandhi: "The weak can never forgive. Forgiveness is the attribute of the strong."

If letting go of the past seems a tall order, it is often because we refuse to be victims of the same behavior over and over, and we certainly have that right. So what we can do is practice a method for assertively asking another person to cease harmful or ineffective behavior. We may choose to avoid potential conflict by not saying anything about these behaviors, but that's like a license for the other person to continue.

Elaina Zuker explored assertiveness in *Mastering Assertiveness Skills*.[24] This method, referred to as I-language assertion, is based on the work of Thomas Gordon[25] and involves making a four-part statement in which you describe:

- **WHEN**—an objective description of the other person's behavior, said without judgment or blame
- **THE EFFECT IS**—how the person's behavior affects you
- **I FEEL**—your feelings, without accusation or blame
- **I'D PREFER**—a description of the behavior you want to see. Instead of "I'd prefer," you may also use, "I'd like" or "I'd want."

Here's how you might use it to assert yourself when a friend or colleague is often late for lunch appointments:

- **WHEN** you arrive late for our lunch appointment,
- **THE EFFECT IS** that we lose our reservations and then have to rush through lunch.
- **I FEEL** anxious about being late for my afternoon appointments and I'm disappointed that we are not able to catch up like we planned.
- **I'D PREFER** that you show up on time or call at least 30 minutes in advance so I can make adjustments.

By describing the other person's behavior without judgment or blame, you are acting assertively. If you had told your lunch partner, "When you're late for lunch, you really make me mad. Who do you think you are? What's wrong with you?" you would have certainly made the person defensive with your blaming, aggressive tone.

This I-language technique will help you determine when your feelings result from some violation of your rights and when they are caused by trying to impose your own values and expectations on others. In describing feelings, remember to state only the effect of the behavior on you. "I feel you are being unfair" is a judgment, not a feeling. Stated properly, I-language feelings can very powerful. We often avoid speaking of feelings because we do not want to put more emotion than necessary into a difficult situation. But you have a right to express your feelings in a constructive manner and, remember, no one can disagree with how you feel.

This model may seem artificial or too complex on initial review. But it is only four short steps, and I urge you to always write out, or at least carefully consider, your words to ensure that you don't sound accusatorial or blaming but speak in a straightforward, practical and constructive way to assert your perspective on things.

Once you have made your assertion, stop talking! Give the other person time to consider what you have said and do not expect an immediate, or any, response. You've made your case and it will be up to the other person to adapt his or her behavior.

Ask yourself:

- Is there a pattern of behavior with another that is hurting our relationship?

- Is this important enough to assert myself?

- Am I willing to prepare what I want to say so it can be done in the most effective manner?

HOW TO TURN POTENTIALLY BAD CONVERSATIONS INTO GOOD ONES

I don't pretend we have all the answers.
But the questions are certainly worth thinking about.
—Arthur C. Clarke

ONE OF THE BETTER BOOKS on building relationships I ever read was *Powerful Conversations: How High Impact Leaders Communicate,* by Phil Harkins. You might be asking, "Don't you mean a book on communicating?" No, because the only way we really build relationships is with truly effective conversations, and we can all work on those to communicate better. Harkins identifies these elements of good conversations:

Helps Build Relationships: It shows you are interested in the other's position and willing to seek win-win solutions.

- Sense of mutual respect
- Active listening, even with differences
- Strengthening the relationship

Assists in Gaining Understanding and Perspective: Only by digging into what is important and meaningful to another can you craft the best solutions for all involved.

- Acceptance, lack of being judged
- Developing shared meaning
- Learning something new or important

Achieves Focus: Good conversations help us find ways to sort through volumes of options and focus on what we can accomplish together.

- Taking the time to reflect on what's important
- Exploring questions that matter
- Strengthening mutual commitment

We have all had conversations where we exchanged valuable insights, built on our mutual understanding and derived excellent options for actions. Such conversations demonstrate that "none of us is as smart as all of us." However, Harkins also acknowledges that the opposite can be true as well: "Bad conversations" can arise.

The "communication vibration" that occurs between the sender of a message and the receiver of the message provides clues about whether the message is getting through. Harkins identifies seven elements of bad conversations,[26] and I have suggested several responses you may use with each to try to turn around the flow of the interaction. With these questions, you are letting the listeners know you would like them to take another approach or continue the conversation later. You'll make better use of each person's time by having a dialogue when all sides are ready to be as constructive and positive as possible.

Unclear, poorly expressed content:

- I'm not sure if I understand the message here. Could you rephrase or repeat that?
- Let me see if I'm clear on your request/statement/observation. What you're saying is . . . . Does that summarize it accurately?
- I'm sorry, but I'm not familiar with that topic/definition/term/ what you mean by _____. Could I ask you to clarify that?

Unfocused content:

- I seem to hear several different issues here. Can we separate and then prioritize them to focus our discussion?
- We were speaking about X originally and now we are talking about Y. Can you tell me how they are related or should we deal with one at a time?
- You've really got a lot of stuff/issues/material here. Could I ask you to break it down into the key points/concerns you want us to address?

Frequent interruptions:

- Could I suggest we close the door/hold the calls while I get a good understanding of this issue?
- You seem to be a more accomplished multitasker than I am. To help me out, could we stick to this one issue right now?
- If this is not a convenient time, let's pick a time that's good for us both. (Use this if things look really out of control when you enter someone else's office)
- It really seems like you've got a lot happening right now. Should we consider rescheduling? (Use this if someone gets interrupted while you are with them or fails to give you full attention)

Unexpressed feelings or beliefs:

- You seem very sure of your position on this issue. What led you to believe that?
- Can you tell me how all this is affecting you (and perhaps your team/group)?
- If I were in your shoes, I might feel angry/frustrated/ disappointed/betrayed/excited/anxious about this situation. How is it affecting you?

- In speaking with others about this situation, what are people's impressions of what's going on and the reasons for it? What are your thoughts?

Unspoken wants and needs:

- If you had no limitations here, what would you want to happen?
- For you (or your team) to really make an impact in this situation, what do you need from the organization/group/team/me?
- It appears no one has asked your opinion on what you would like to see happen here. Can you give me your suggestions?

Harsh voice and tone:

- I can tell from the intensity of your voice that you are upset/angry/disappointed/frustrated. Is this going to be a good time to speak about this or should we find another?
- The words you are choosing to characterize our teammates/the other group/function will not help us in thinking through to a win-win solution.

Inconsistent, nonverbal signals or unresponsive body language:

- I don't think I am making myself clear. Can I clarify anything for you?
- Based upon my reading of your body language, it appears that I am not able to be very convincing. Do you want to continue this discussion or think about it some more? Can we schedule a time to reconvene (if they decide to think about it)?
- You appear, just based on your body language, to dismiss my suggestions/to be upset by my ideas/to reject my position. What can we do to make this conversation more productive?

These responses can help turn around conversations that are headed in the wrong direction.

Ask yourself:

- Can I find ways to ensure that the elements of good conversations are in evidence in most of my interactions with others?

- Reflecting on a bad conversation I recently had, can I identify which of the seven possible causes were responsible for getting it off track?

- Am I willing to study these seven causes and the potential responses to add to my repertoire of verbal skills to enhance my reputation as a good conversationalist?

The Art of the Joke

I love people who make me laugh. I honestly think it's the thing
I like most, to laugh. It cures a multitude of ills.
It's probably the most important thing in a person.
—Audrey Hepburn

I RECENTLY HEARD THAT a couple of clients of mine were challenged because their attempts at using humor in meetings were often not well received. I admire someone who can tell a good joke. My father was excellent at telling jokes and humorous stories and developed the craft throughout his life. I learned how to tell jokes by observing him and we often started our conversations by sharing the best jokes we had heard recently. My father had the timing, the memory and the voice for telling a great joke, and he followed his punchlines with a hearty, infectious laugh that showed he was enjoying the experience and the joke all over again each time he told it and drew others into the merriment.

My father died a dozen years ago, and in his things I discovered a little book filled with the punchlines to jokes. Just the punchlines! There were 40 pages of his neat printing to remind him of jokes. Dad could tell a "blue" joke or might make fun of some folks, but his jokes were rarely ever mean, vulgar or inappropriate for the setting. Most were clever, involved good word play and always invited the listener in to enjoy the moment. His purpose was to unleash a little goodwill and help everyone have some fun.

If you want to get good at telling jokes, you should:

- Write down what you heard to help you remember it.
- Practice saying it many times to get the timing down.
- Imagine how those you are telling it to will respond, trying to anticipate any negative response.

I practice new jokes to myself as I am walking or driving. The cardinal sin of telling a joke is to forget a punch line, and you can avoid that only with practice and repetition. Great comedians will often show up at a club and do an impromptu few minutes to "test" a joke to gauge reactions.

I came across an interesting article on the web by Michael Moffa, "The Danger of Joking at Work: The Rise and Fall of Workplace Humor."[27] Moffa says, "Americans take great pride in being special, smart, egalitarian, friendly, casual, open, successfully competitive, extroverted, belonging, take-charge, popular, playful, powerful and self-assertive. Telling a joke enables them to accomplish every one of these in one go."

I am not sure if anyone consciously considers these reasons when injecting humor in a workplace discussion, and I am for as much levity as possible in any group of people, but here are my suggestions if you decide to liven things up with humor:

1. Be aware of your audience. Some humor does not translate from culture to culture. Keep in mind that we live in a multicultural world.

2. Why are you injecting humor? If your comments are insensitive, at another's expense or could be misconstrued, don't make them.

3. Do not let your humorous comments sidetrack a discussion.

4. If you are telling a joke or story, be sure you have it well prepared. Practice!

5. Scan the room or group to get a sense of how others might react. You need to anticipate how receptive the audience is so you'll get the reaction you're looking for.

6. Avoid inside jokes, so those who will not understand the meaning or context won't feel left out.

Many people respond humorously or cleverly "off the top of their heads." They are naturals at using a lighter touch, but even if you're not naturally quick-witted, you can learn some aspects of injecting humor in your interactions with others and in presentations before groups. Here's a joke that's easy to remember. You have my permission to borrow it, if only for practice.

A 93-year-old woman was being interviewed in the seniors' facility in which she resided. The television reporter asked her why, at her advanced age, she had decided to get married for the fourth time. The woman responded that she had outlived her first three husbands and enjoyed the companionship. When asked about her husbands, she mentioned that the first had been a banker; the second was a circus performer; and the third was a preacher. Her new husband's family owned several funeral parlors. So she said that when she thought about her married life, it was "one for the money, two for the show, three to get ready and four to go."

Ask yourself:

- If I use humor at work, does it help or hurt the quality of the discussions I'm in?

- If I want to tell a good joke or story, am I willing to prepare to deliver it well?

- If I know someone whose humor I admire, will I buy them a cup of coffee and ask them about how they use their humor?

Slaying the Email Beast

Email, instant messaging, and cell phones give us fabulous communication ability, but because we live and work in our own little worlds, that communication is totally disorganized.
—Marilyn vos Savant

For communication to occur there must be a sender and a receiver. Until the sender gets a response from the receiver of the message, the communication link is incomplete. Although email is a highly efficient data transmission tool, it is not the most effective mode of communication. In fact, most of us are overwhelmed with email and other data.

Several years ago I conducted a survey for a highly successful international investment banking team to better understand the impact of email communications on their team, especially regarding the time they spent using email and the perceived benefits. Some of the key findings from this team of more than 200 people:

- Seventy percent spent more than 20 hours a week on email.
- They spent 1.4 hours per evening and 1.65 hours per weekend on email.
- Ninety-two percent of people said others were distracted by multitasking when you spoke to them.
- Eighty-four percent responded to email constantly or "whenever I get a chance."

I offered several suggestions for improving things (email dos and don'ts below) but they still have challenges with email.

Several folks who work with a client of mine who is a prolific user of email said his emails were intrusive and overwhelming. One woman got six emails on Mother's Day and another stopped responding to him after hours and on weekends. Others were intimidated when they got email from him at 3 or 4 a.m. Is there an implied duty to respond ASAP to one of the senior leaders of your company? This email dilemma creates its own set of pressures and challenges in the workplace. On August 28, 2014, *The New York Times*[28] had a commentary by Clive Thompson titled "End the Tyranny of 24/7 Email." Here are some chilling facts from that article:

- White-collar workers spend 28 percent of their time on email and check messages 74 times a day.
- White-collar workers who use smart phones are "umbilically connected to email a stunning 13.5 hours per day" and 38 percent check email even during dinner.

Some companies are trying to combat this menace. Daimler, the German automaker, allows employees to set their corporate email to "holiday mode" when they are on vacation. The email directs senders to an alternate person who can assist them. Then the email messages are deleted so employees do not have to come back to an avalanche of email to catch up on.

The Toronto office of Edelman, the global public relations firm, created a "7-to-7" rule to strongly discourage email before 7 a.m. or after 7 p.m. Employees can check email if they want, but they are not supposed to send it to colleagues. If there is a client crisis, any employee is free to use their judgment to respond as they see fit. And that last part—using their judgment—is critical.

When people send email for every little detail they can think of, to inform every member of the task force on all issues big and small, it reflects a lack of confidence and empowerment on the part of everyone, Thompson cautions. He states:

". . . when employees are actually empowered, they make more judgment calls on their own. They also start using phone calls and face-to-face chats to resolve issues quickly, so they don't metastasize into email threads the length of *War and Peace.* This is basic behavioral economics. When email is seen as an infinite resource, people abuse it. If a corporation constrains its use, each message becomes more valuable—and employees become more mindful of how and when they write."

Such a change does not need to be a draconian policy. Employees like to have the flexibility to check email on their timetable. But email policies must come from the top and be enforced from the top down. This will NOT bubble up from the troops because there are too many risks in taking on this thorny issue. If you value employee engagement in an atmosphere where there is still a lot of fear about job security generally, this is one policy change you may wish to consider.

Here are some tips to help you and your staff increase the value of the time spent on email:

Email Dos:

- Pick up the phone or schedule a phone call if your emails go back and forth more than two or three times on a topic. You'll get more accomplished.
- Say what you need in the subject line. In the subject line write (choose one): 1) Subject—FYI, or (2) Subject—Action required and by when, or (3) Subject—Response required and by when.
- If you send email to several people at the same time, identify who is to act or respond to the message. This will minimize confusion about who has accountability.
- Use numbers in the subject line. They get attention and give the reader an understanding of the breadth of what you are asking. For example: "2 Things to Consider for Tomorrow's Meeting," "4 Days left to Prepare Our Report or "Quarterly Review" or "3 Essentials for the Budget Submission." Using a number encourages people to read because they want to know what the number of things might be. It also seems more manageable when it's a small number.

- Try to process emails fully when you read them. If the response takes two minutes or less, get it done. If you need to work on them or are waiting for a response, you can move the inbox items to folders labeled "@action" or "@pending." You probably do a good job of placing paper documents in such proper folders. Do it with email. The @ symbol should keep those emails at the top of any list you may have.
- Be judicious about using the urgent tag in email. If everything is urgent, nothing is urgent!
- Block out time to check email and voice mail several times during the day. Consider this batch processing time. Use the time to review calls and email and prioritize the responses needed. If you have set aside time for yourself, block it off in your calendar and get in the habit of using that time as you planned. Remember, if you can repeat a behavior for at least 21 days in a row, you greatly enhance the ability to make it a habit that will stick.
- Unsubscribe to as much as you can. All those interesting newsletters or other things you once thought might be great to look at when you had some down time are a real waste of your time. They clog up your inbox, and you have more important things to do.
- Think about how the receivers you are sending your messages to prefer to get communications. You can always ask them. Just because email works for you does not mean it is effective for everyone else. Others may want a text message or phone call.
- Track how long you spend on email at the office, in the evening, on weekends and while traveling. It can be a time sinkhole.
- Start longer emails by telling the reader what you want in response. A little note early on ("Can you double check the numbers below?") will allow them to focus their thoughts as they read.

Email Don'ts:

- Don't even think of looking at email for the first hour of the workday. Email can crowd out time for planning and preparing. Don't get stuck in a reactive mode. Decide the night before the most important thing you should get done the next day. Spend the first hour organizing and preparing to complete that task.

- Don't use the "Reply to All" response. It clogs up the email system, especially when it's a congratulations or "atta boy." Pick up the phone and call instead.

- Don't send an email if you are upset or angry. You may use words or tone that you'll regret. Since you don't get immediate feedback when you draft an email, like you might during a live conversation or even over the phone, you are not as temperate as you might be. You'll avoid trouble if you leave the email as a draft and review it when you are not upset or emotional.

- Don't send email late at night when you are tired. You can get sloppy or curt when you're tired. Leave the email as a draft and send it in the morning.

- Don't act like Pavlov's dog and respond immediately to every email. Turn off the sound or vibration email notification on your desktop computer and your phone. Respond in a manner that does not compound the distractions that surround you.

Ask yourself:

- How much time do I devote to email in the office? How much after hours?

- What policies could we adopt to wean the team from bad email habits?

- Where in my daily schedule can I block time for email so I don't become enslaved to responding to email throughout the day?

Resources for further ideas

Julie Morgenstern. *Organizing from the Inside Out.* (New York, NY: Henry Holt and Company) 1998.

David Allen. *Getting Things Done: The Art of Stress-Free Productivity.* (New York, NY: Penguin Group) 2001.

David Allen. *Ready for Anything: 52 Productivity Principles for Getting Things Done,* (New York, NY: Penguin Group) 2003.

Avoiding Communication Breakdowns

Communication breakdown.
It's always the same.
I'm having a nervous breakdown.
Drive me insane!
— "Communications Breakdown" by rock band Led Zeppelin

When you think about some of challenges in your business communications, do you experience frustration and angst? It happens to everyone from time to time. It rarely causes insanity but can make you ask yourself whether the message that was received was what you intended. There can be technical or cultural reasons for miscommunication. People can be too busy or messages get lost in the avalanche of information coming their way. People may disagree and not know how to handle disagreements well. The possibilities are numerous, but consider some of the most common causes for breakdowns and solutions that may produce more productive dialogue.

A large part of any miscommunication will always center on the communication vehicle you choose. Here are the three basic choices: face-to-face conversations, telephone conversations and email. Each of these has its pros and cons, but I believe there are two variables that matter the most: efficiency and effectiveness. Here's a graphic depiction of the overall communication process that illustrates where some of the key differences are in communicating our messages to others:

Communication Breakdown

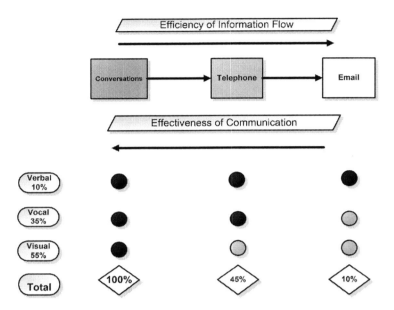

Email: Regarding efficiency, email, texts, Twitter and other technologies will win hands down over snail mail or phone calls, much less face-to-face meetings. The latter take more time to organize or it's just difficult to catch people because of busy schedules and geographical separation, whether it's different floors, cities, states or even continents. It is really amazing how much information can be transmitted electronically, and the cold reality of being overwhelmed by the email beast is a result. Perhaps there can be too much of a good thing.

Telephone: Today smart phones are ubiquitous. They enable so much more than just phone calls. I am frequently dismayed to see couples at a nice restaurant who have their eyes on their phones rather than speaking to each other. But phone conversations can be useful in creating real-time dialogue that allows a good back-and-forth as opposed to responding to the words in an email and then waiting for a response.

Face-to-Face Conversations: Personal conversations have an immediacy and impact that allow more effective communication to occur, but in the global environment we operate in, these get harder and harder to schedule. Even companies with worldwide operations see the value of bringing key leaders together in person at least once a year.

Elements of the Communications Exchange

The challenge is that the effectiveness of the communications exchange is the opposite of its efficiency. The difference in the communications exchange has to do with the clarity of the meaning that is intended and that which is received. In face-to-face communications, it is important to know that studies have shown that there are three elements that establish the communication "vibration" that results from successful interactions:

Verbal: Verbal cues are the words that are used in communication. In our increasingly global environment, there is a lot of room for misunderstanding about various words or phrases between cultures, even when someone's native language is the same as yours. Note the differences in English terms used in Great Britain and the United States for the same thing. Even here in the U.S., just think of how many meanings there are for the word "fast": "Fast" cars, paint that holds "fast," a knot that holds "fast," "fast" women, refraining from eating—a "fast." The real issue is that the words themselves are only 10 percent of the communication "vibration," which I describe as the net message the receiver gets from the sender of the message. You may scoff at this figure but many extensive studies bear this out. For example, Albert Mehrabian's *Nonverbal Communication* (Chicago, IL: Aldine Transaction, 2007).

Vocal: Vocal cues involve the tone, pace and often the volume of the speaker. The vocal aspects of any communication "vibration" account for 35 percent of the message.

- **Tone** can be heard in inflections, emphasis or the passion or other emotions the speaker is demonstrating.
- **Pace** often reflects the fact that people tend to speed up when they are excited or animated about a topic and slow down or become more deliberate when the situation is more serious or reflective.
- **Volume** can vary, but when people are enthusiastic about a topic they often speak louder and more emphatically. The inverse may be also true; in an animated discussion, a speaker may purposely reduce volume to create contrast.

Visual: An astounding 55 percent of communication comes from the visual, or what you see in others during an interpersonal exchange. You may think that is an unrealistically high figure, but scientific studies have substantiated this since the 1950s. Facial features, especially the eyes and the mouth, convey a great deal without words. For example, rolling of the eyes and compressed lips may reflect holding back emotions. An individual's body language is also a great source of insight. How people hold their arms, lean into you when they speak or demonstrate they are following along with you when you speak are also critical to understanding this part of the "vibration." Here's what you're faced with in terms of the communications choices:

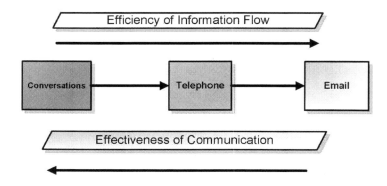

The chance for the clearest and most complete communication is going to be with face-to-face conversations or in meeting situations where you can experience the verbal, vocal and visual aspects of the communication vibration. Unfortunately, that isn't very practical in this increasingly globally distributed world we work in. So here are a few tips to consider to improve the effectiveness of your communication:

- Email is efficient but not always effective. If you've gone back and forth more than three or four times in an email string, pick up the phone and chat with your email recipient. You may even have to set up a phone call, but you'll pick up so much more in the communication that it will be worth it.

- Although there is a generational trend that sees smart phones as more for email and text messages than for phone calls, consider leaving a voicemail to convey your message better or to ask to schedule a call or meeting. In some organizations, voicemail is not a preferred method of communicating, but you can leave an email to give the receiver of your message a heads up that something important could be on that voicemail that you can't, or would rather not, convey in an email.

- Where practical, make sure you maintain your preference for meeting in person and connecting where you can get 100 percent of the communication vibration. Skype, Face Time messaging and videoconferencing are increasingly available and are the next best thing to meeting in person. It may require a little more planning but is relatively cost-effective and usually worth it.

- When you are developing ongoing relationships with important clients or coworkers, ask them their preferred method of getting messages.

Breakdowns in the communication "vibration," the net message between the sender and receiver, can occur for many reasons, so you must work constantly to improve communication skills.

Ask yourself:

- What can I do to maximize the opportunity to get the verbal, vocal and visual aspects in my communications?

- Since the visual, or body language, aspects of the communication vibration are so important, what can I do to learn more about this to enhance my effectiveness as a leader?

DEALING WITH THE ELEPHANTS:
WHY WE FAIL TO CONFRONT THE OBVIOUS

Everyone stumbles over the truth from time to time, but most people pick themselves up and hurry off as though nothing ever happened.
— WINSTON CHURCHILL

HAVE YOU EVER LEFT a meeting and said to yourself, "Why didn't they talk about Subject X? That's really what the problem is." So why didn't you bring it up?

The commonplace hesitance to address the existence of the "elephant in the room" is described in the book *The Elephant in the Room: Silence and Denial in Everyday Life* by Eviatar Zerubavel.[29]

In the context of everyday organizational life, there are some issues that no one wants to raise or discuss. For whatever reasons, people tend to avoid dealing with issues that need to be discussed rather than ignored.

It may often feel like this is a matter of inertia, but Zerubavel says, ". . . as the foremost expression of co-denial, silence is a collective endeavor, and it involves a collaborative effort on the parts of both the potential generator and recipient of a given piece of information to stay away from it. A conspiracy of silence presupposes discretion on the part of the non-producer of the information as well as inattention on the part of its non-consumers." (p. 48)

So people act with discretion for various reasons in not dealing with key issues that may need to be discussed; others in the same meeting either are not paying attention or gloss over the issue.

Not paying attention is obviously a poor excuse for not thinking through or discussing key issues, but purposely avoiding them is another problem altogether. Zerubavel maintains, "In other words, the very act of avoiding the elephant is itself an elephant! Not only do we avoid it, we do so without acknowledging that we are actually doing so, thereby denying our denial." (p. 53)

So what causes this issue to repeat itself in organizational life everywhere? Here are some reasons you may have encountered for not identifying the elephant in the room:

1. No one but me seems to be aware of the issue or is concerned about it. If I chose to raise it, I could be:

- Embarrassed. They may all have a common history of the issue, common experience, organization, product or personal knowledge that I do not. It may be a non-issue for them.
- Misinformed. I have bad or out-of-date info or perhaps I didn't read all the data before the meeting.
- Labeled a nonconformist. We don't do things like that in this company. We are too nice to point out issues or concerns like that.
- Showboating or grandstanding. It might seem as if I am bringing this up because I am seeking to draw attention to myself, to how smart I am.
- Seen as a naysayer. People may think I'm just being negative and holding things up.

2. I'm afraid.

- Will bringing up the issue affect my reputation and my ability to get other jobs in the company?
- How could speaking out affect my bonus or merit increase?
- Will calling attention to the issue make me more vulnerable to being let go or laid off?

3. It's not worth it right now.

- My input might throw off the time line that's been committed to. It's too late to do anything about it now.
- I am not sure the leaders really want more input now.
- My suggestion is a "nice to have" rather than a "have to have." It could create or add things that slow the project down.

4. It seems radioactive.

- It calls into doubt another's veracity, inconsistent position or self-serving motives.
- It reflects badly on another's ethics, morals, view of the issue or intellectual capacity.

The Emperor's New Clothes

Many often consider the elephant in the room concept along with "The Emperor's New Clothes," a clever fable that was written in 1837. The two men who weave these marvelous clothes come to town and make it very clear that ". . . the clothes made of their material possessed the wonderful quality of being invisible to any man who was unfit for his office or unpardonably stupid."

What a wicked conceit! And they were very vocal about this qualification. So no one wanted to be found unfit for office or unpardonably stupid and, thus, went along with the charade. People were reluctant to speak up!

The child in the story was both unaware and unconcerned with being found out. He was just a child, so he said what he saw. How do we get ourselves and our organizations to speak like the child and say the obvious? It is difficult to do. Before it can happen, those people party to conspiracies of silence must be ready to hear the proverbial child's announcement that the emperor has no clothes. Yet as Enron's Sherron Watkins found out when she told

175

Chairman Kenneth Lay that their company's accounting methods were improper, she underestimated management's unwillingness to address the issue.

Like whistle-blowers, silence breakers are often ridiculed, vilified and ostracized. Aside from their immediate punitive function, such retaliatory tactics are also designed to intimidate anybody else who contemplates breaking the conspiracy of silence, which indeed prevents many potential silence breakers from actually doing so. (p.72)

Because whistle-blowers and silence-breakers often catch upper management off guard, organizations usually react without a systematic plan to stifle independent thought, but the response can be punitive. Many executives go from meeting to meeting with very little preparation. Some of the reasons for ignoring the elephant are related more to the multitasking work world than to any thoughtful or calculated response. We fail to pay attention and just try to get through the day and go on to the next meeting. This may explain the failure to acknowledge problems, but it does not excuse it.

Part of the reason we resent silence breakers is that… they disturb cognitive tranquility. Even more important, they try to force us to acknowledge things we specifically choose to ignore to avoid getting hurt or upset. (p.74)

This is especially true when the cultural norm may be to not "rock the boat" or challenge people, assumptions or processes. The problem is that better ways of doing things are not discussed, ongoing concerns are not resolved and creativity and innovation are diminished.

Behavior that is inconsistent with organizational values can also continue unchecked. So beyond the opportunity to continuously improve the organization, which can be stifled, not confronting "bad" behavior or ideas can create a cynical reaction to the professed values of the organization that weakens and erodes them.

Like so many other things in life, it comes down to courage!

Potential Solutions

So how do we deal with these elephants? How do we say the emperor is naked in a constructive but forceful manner? Here are some suggestions:

Personalize the discussion in a constructive manner and allow appropriate dialogue. This forces the group to be empathic to the impact of what they are doing:

- "At this time, should we consider the impact of this decision upon…?"
- "Perhaps we should think of the implications of this for (state the individual, entity, process, client, etc.)."
- "Is it useful for us to reflect upon any unintended consequences of this decision?"
- Play a little dumb to be able to raise the issue or perspective you think is needed:
  - "I may be missing something here, but …"
  - "I may be way off base here, but …"
- Create permission for someone else to comment:
  - "What's the argument against this …?"
  - "What might a client think about this …?"
  - "Has anyone considered …?"

Set up the opportunity for discussion of the "elephant" in the next meeting by:

- Discussing it with the meeting leader and getting it on the agenda
- Asking other key partners in the company about their thoughts about the issue and suggestions for next steps

Ask yourself:
- Am I willing to confront the elephant in the room when needed?

- Will I try some of the suggestions listed in the potential solutions above?
- I may have reasons to protect myself and my career, but how real or significant are the risks I'm worried about?

TRIANGULATION:
DON'T GET CAUGHT IN THE MIDDLE

Any problem, big or small, within a family always seems to start with
bad communication. Someone isn't listening.

—EMMA THOMPSON

IN A CHURCH SERVICE RECENTLY, the biblical reading was from Matthew 18: 15-17: "If your brother sins against you, go and tell him his fault, between you and him alone. If he listens to you, you have gained your brother. But if he does not listen, take one or two others along with you, that every charge may be established by the evidence of two or three witnesses. If he refuses to listen to them, tell it to the church."

The minister referred to a communication concept called triangulation that brings currency and relevance in interpreting these biblical verses. I often refer to the concept of triangulation in discussions about communication dysfunctions with my clients. Here's a graphical depiction of triangulation:

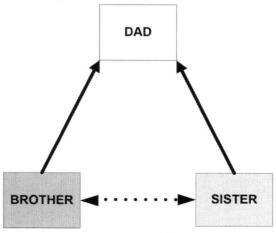

Let's say that two siblings have a serious disagreement about a family matter. They are frustrated with each other and their respective positions. Often the siblings will express their frustration to a neutral third party—in this case Dad (or Mom). They are looking for support and acknowledgment for themselves and their rationale for their position.

This triangle also represents the reality of what professional counselors or therapists do in their role as "dad." They are trained to give people perspective and support in dealing with their challenges. They may also bring in both parties to assist in their discussion or mediate between them. But remember, they are trained to do this and have to be as objective about things as they possibly can be.

But parents in this kind of situation often want to help both sides. A good mediator must push the issue back to the brother and sister before he weighs in, having them share the concern and hopefully reach some resolution between themselves first.

The brother or sister must go to the other first and hold them accountable and seek resolution about the matter before discussing it with another. Now emotions may be running high but it is unfair to "dump the dispute on a third party, putting them in an awkward or uncomfortable position." The "dumper" is exploiting the other person, the "dumpee." The dumper may just be looking for a sympathetic ear and some personal reassurance, but nothing will get resolved until brother and sister actually hash this out between them.

Be Neither a "Dumper" nor a "Dumpee."

Here are some recommendations to prevent getting sucked into the snare of triangulation:

1. Calm down before you approach anyone. Don't allow your emotions to permit you to express yourself in anger or frustration.

2. Although you may wish to solicit insights from another to test your perspectives or reasoning, do not ask them to take your side.

3. Find time to go directly to the other party to resolve the issue. Charles Kettering, the "genius of G.M.", once said, "A problem well stated is a problem half solved." So seek to:

- Establish the facts in this situation,
- Discuss different perspectives and seek options for reconciling your differences,
- Agree on a resolution, or
- Seek a third party to help mediate your dispute.

Your reputation should be a reflection of how you resolve issues just as much as what outcomes occur. If you cannot reach an agreement and the issue is substantive enough, then raise it to an appropriate person who you both believe can be effective at helping you sort through things.

Each side needs to be accountable for how they behave in disputes. If you can agree that you will both abide by the decision reached, that is a real plus. I have seen people say unkind things about another who was not there to represent their side of the story.

Ask yourself:

- Do I go directly to others I need to deal with or do I complain to others about them instead?

- Am I willing to stop being a "dumper"?

- Do I know how to protect myself from being a "dumpee," having others drag me in to disputes in an inappropriate way? (See: Using I-Language Assertiveness in Your Interactions)

ARE YOU AFRAID OF TALKING TO YOURSELF?

The single biggest problem in communication
is the illusion that it has taken place.
—GEORGE BERNARD SHAW

WHEN YOU ASK SOMEONE how things are going, how often do you hear "Super!"? If your experience is like mine, there is usually one word that follows "Super" and that is "busy." I also hear "insanely busy" or "ridiculously busy." Are we actually that busy? For many people the answer is, sadly, yes.

We fill our time with work, exercise, errands and other duties and leave very little time for contemplation, reflection or just pondering. I recently saw a very attractive couple at dinner and both were looking intently at their smartphones rather than conversing. The 18-year-old son of my golf partner was intent on looking at his phone prior to stepping up to the tee box on almost every hole. And this was on a gorgeous Saturday morning. Now all of them might have had important things to keep track of, but none of them was in the moment in what I considered wonderful surroundings.

In a *New York Times* (July 27, 2014) article, "No Time To Think," Kate Murphy mentioned that a psychology professor at the University of Virginia, Timothy Wilson, conducted 11 experiments involving more than 700 people and found that the majority of participants reported that they found it unpleasant to be alone in a room with their own thoughts for just six to 15 minutes. It didn't matter if they were at home or in the laboratory, they just didn't like "being in their own heads."

One of Murphy's suggestions was that one of the reasons we do not like to be in our own heads is that the problems we are confronting in life frequently seem to come to the forefront. In a society "which values doing more than thinking and believes answers are in the palm of your hand rather than in your own head," she asks, "is it any wonder that we avoid the deliberate processes of reflection or contemplation?" If we see ourselves as active problem solvers, we tend to devalue the process of playing "what if." Evasion or deferral of dealing with such challenges by engaging in extreme busyness actually can make problems worse over time because of this conscious neglect.

In some regards, it seems to me that this is often a generational issue. My 20-something children could never seem to understand why I didn't have music blasting in my ears wherever I went. But I actually like to be in my own head and often random but significant insights crop up on long walks. I sometimes carry a small pocket recorder to capture these ideas. But as my kids point out, I am a dinosaur.

Murphy also mentions that lack of reflection can impair your ability to empathize with others. She quotes Giancarlo DiMaggio of the Center for Metacognitive Interpersonal Therapy in Rome: "The more in touch with my own feelings and experiences, the richer and more accurate are my guesses of what passes through another person's mind. Feeling what you feel is an ability that atrophies if you don't use it." There is a significant correlation between empathy and success as an executive. Your ability to understand the needs or issues of someone you are communicating or negotiating with will enhance the quality of that communication and your ability to create win-win outcomes.

To effectively take advantage of what empathy can do for you in making your communications more effective, step back after a challenging conversation and contemplate what happened according to the diagram on the next page.

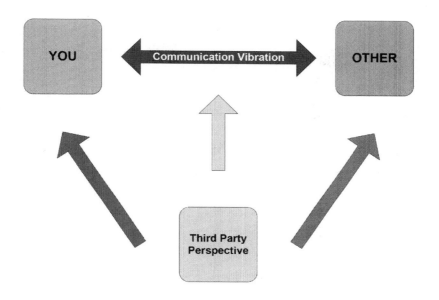

Imagine you were on the outside looking in, watching the interaction between yourself and someone else, taking the third-party perspective. Granted, this is hard to do because we are biased in our perspectives, but truly empathic people can develop this emotional intelligence skill. A communication "vibration" occurs between you and the other person—a combination of the words, the vocal expression and the nonverbal signals between you.

You will never get to this critical reflection if you can't put down your phone or won't take the time—maybe just for 90 seconds! Don't allow yourself to be too busy to think!

Ask yourself:

- What was accomplished with this communication?

- Does either of us feel good about this interaction?

- Did I feel I not only heard what they said but have a good feel for why it is important to them? (That does not mean you agree, just that you understand.)

- Do I feel they heard and understood me?

- If a stranger had listened to us speaking, what would he or she think about the quality and effectiveness of our communication and relationship?

CHANGE

INTRO: THE CHALLENGE OF CHANGE

I BELIEVE THAT MANAGING CHANGE needs to be a key focus for managers, and especially leaders, who are often charged with initiating and leading change to assist their organizations to adapt, grow and thrive in an ever-changing world. *Fortune* magazine maintains a list of the top 500 companies in the United States. In 2014, the 500th had revenues of almost $5 billion and a market capitalization of $8 billion—and it was last. But of the companies that made 1999's *Fortune* 500 list, 238 would disappear in just 10 years, acquired, merged or broken into pieces.

Early in my career I worked for the RCA Corporation until it was acquired by General Electric. The RCA brand—once a leader in many products—is just a memory today. And this kind of change happens at an ever-accelerating pace. I recently read an article about business velocity that stated 45 percent to 70 percent of the total profits for a new videogame were often accumulated in just the first four to five days of sales. That's days!

The inevitability and magnitude of change in so many markets leads to unprecedented levels of disruption, reinvention and renewal. We see this in political, social, economic and religious trends across the globe. Change is often painful, but no one can ignore it and no one should avoid preparing for it.

The topics in this section deal with anticipating the emotional and psychological reactions to change we see in the folks we interact with, primarily with a focus on those we lead. I will not be discussing the process of leading a large-scale change effort for several reasons. First, such major change efforts very frequently fail—usually because of resistance from those who are being asked to change and the ineffectiveness of those leading the change process. This doesn't mean that change should be avoided, but many people simply underestimate the complexity and challenge of leading a successful change effort.

I have seen a wide variety of key, large-scale organizational change in my career. Much of the literature on organizational change reflects the huge emphasis placed on designing the products, the structure or the promotion of the change at hand. But the actual management of the change process usually gets short shrift. I believe this happens because many organizations either do not know or understand the critical elements of leading a change process well or are not willing to commit the people or the investment to make it happen well.

In his book, *The First 90 Days: Critical Success Strategies for New Leaders at All Levels,*[30] Michael Watkins provides an excellent model for a large-scale, complex organizational change (on next page).

In my experience, many organizations are neither equipped nor willing to commit the time to prepare for and execute on such a thorough model. Like many things that I see relating to people in organizations, such efforts are considered to be costs that are to be managed and minimized rather than investments that can create a robust return on investment. But that's a larger challenge to deal with. So let's concentrate on those change elements that, with increased understanding and appreciation, you can anticipate, plan for and execute with much higher levels of effectiveness.

Although Watkins' model carefully details how a complex organizational change can be well managed, I intend to focus on the emotional and psychological impact of change in the change process. I intend to do this for several reasons:

- Change is somewhat predictable—not the ability to predict exactly *what* will happen, in which case I'd spend my days placing bets in Las Vegas, but *how* people react to change does seem to follow some predictable scripts.
- Emotional reactions to change drive people's behavior, and as a leader that is what you have to respond to.

FRAMEWORK FOR MANAGING CHANGE

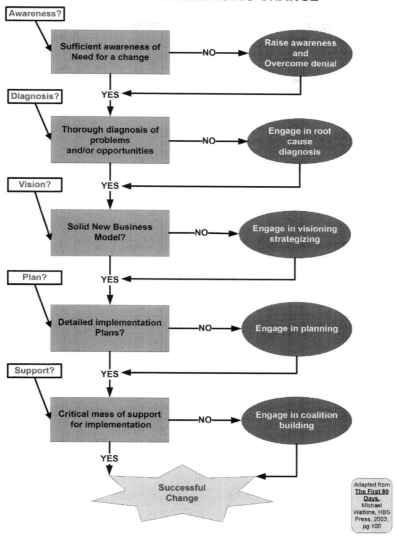

Adapted from **The First 90 Days**, Michael Watkins, HBS Press, 2003, pg.100

- The benefit of a way to systematically analyze and potentially predict reactions to change should enhance your ability to understand how these changes are affecting you as well. You must lead yourself first.

- A change initiative that is well led can reinvigorate an organization. Unfortunately, a poorly led one can not only waste money and market position but also cause people to flee.

The problem with change begins because human beings are creatures of habit. When we are confronted with different people, routines or expectations, we can feel challenged or even frightened by them. It is this response that we to try work through when faced with a significant change personally or professionally.

A major influence on my understanding of the process of organizational change was the work of William Bridges in his book *Managing Transitions: Making the Most of Change.*[31] I will highlight some key insights from this enlightening book and use examples from my own work in recent years. To begin with, Bridges reflected on the historical way that organizational changes often have been considered. The leaders of an organization or a team make decisions and announce that on a certain date, those changes would take place. So the old situation would *end* on a particular day and the new structure, process or leaders would *begin* on another day. Many companies have their own internal processes for ensuring that these organizational announcements are made in a consistent and timely fashion. The preparatory work to line up the people, process or structure is done in anticipation of this announcement.

So in a very simplistic way, it was thought that things ended on a Friday and then began anew the following Monday. People were often given several days to prepare for the new situation, and internal discussions and deliberations supported that process. What Bridges determined was that the change process was actually more complicated than that, and he indicated that the *transition* phase between beginnings and endings was where the complications for organizational change actually occurred.

I'd like to take you through a brief description of each of the three phases of his change model: endings, transitions and beginnings.

Endings

THE CHANGE MODEL

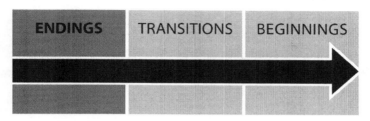

- Endings are what is left behind, what ceases to be.
- Endings are typically viewed as either loss or gain.
- Losses include loss of:
  ROLES • RESPONSIBILITY • CONTROL • EXPERTISE

Adapted from William Bridges, Managing Transitions, Cambridge, MA, DaCapo Press, 1991, 2003

Simply put, endings are what are left behind, what ceases to be. It could be a former team you were a member of, a boss you enjoyed working for, a company you worked for or even a place where you used to gather with friends or work associates. We confront such endings all the time. We tend to accommodate a little more easily those endings that we have no power over or that seem to be the natural order of progress.

But the reality is people usually view endings as either a loss or a gain for themselves personally. I know we would always like to hope that people would put the organization or the team ahead of personal interests, but that is not an accurate reflection of reality. People always engage in a very personal calculus about how any change affects them. To hope for any other perspective is unrealistic.

These losses can include the change of a role or particular job, certain responsibilities, control over all or part of a business operation or even the recognition that a person's technical or professional expertise has become eclipsed by new technologies or systems.

I was in an organization where a new CEO inadvertently denigrated a system that the organization had created over many years. While it was true that the system needed substantial upgrades and improvements, all those individuals who were party to the development of the old system were offended at his tactless repudiation of their work. Although everyone understood the system needed to be further developed and improved, the system they had developed had brought the organization to its current state. There is an old folk saying from the South, "You gotta dance with the one that brung ya," that you owe at least one dance to your date. There is never any reason to do anything but give due deference to those who preceded you and their contributions.

So this reinforces the reality that although people may intellectually understand the need for change, they may have such a significant emotional attachment to the previous situation that the emotional will trump the intellectual. This appears to others as a reluctance to let go of the old ways of doing things and is often perceived as resistance to change. The problem is that when it comes to emotions, everyone reacts differently and in various degrees. This is what makes us human and makes the management of the change process as complicated as it is.

Resistance to change can manifest itself in various ways, both passive and active. On an interpersonal level, passive resistance can include rumors, negative water cooler chatting, leaving people off of communications or folks just ignoring each other. On the active side it can be disruptive behavior in meetings, conscious use of old systems or protocols rather than new ones and many forms of negative nonverbal communication.

It is important that leaders recognize that people will almost always have feelings of loss and that it is going to take both time and understanding to help them move through change. This brings us to the next phase of the change model, transitions, which I refer to as the "neutral zone."

Transitions

THE CHANGE MODEL

- The key is to help people make the link between the old and the new; you can't bypass this stage.
- The three feelings that keep people stuck in transition are:

UNCERTAINTY • MISTRUST • SELF-PRESERVATION

Adapted from William Bridges, Managing Transitions. Cambridge, MA, DaCapo Press, 1991, 2003

Bridges also refers to this phase as the "wilderness" or "neutral zone." In many regards, this is what I find the most remarkable insight that Bridges provided to the knowledge base of change management. What he says is that even though the old organization chart that was in effect on Friday might be eclipsed by the new one that took its place on Monday, everyone goes through an unavoidable period of adapting to whatever the new reality is. It affects everybody in substantially different ways and, thus, there is no real way to predict how everyone will react.

The transitions phase is just that—a period of movement from what was to what will be. The Japanese actually have a name for this concept that does not exist in the English language or, rather, in the American experience. They have a concept called "ma," which refers to an interval that gives shape to the whole. It's often thought of conceptually as a necessary pause between what was and what will be, such as intervals between musical notes or even spaces between words in poems.

In our society, when we have a pause or a gap, what do we do? Are we patient and wait for insight or inspiration to show us the way? No, even if the situation calls for patience, we rush to fill the gap because of our impatience and our internal insistence on action rather than reflection. Since people don't necessarily move through this transition phase in lockstep, what happens? I like to refer to the various creations that bubble up in people's reaction to the change process during these times of uncertainty as "catastrophic fantasies." These are the rumors and innuendos that float around during the transitional phase. Everyone hears them and they often seem pretty crazy or even unhinged. But our impatience causes us to latch on to any potential certainty even if it's a really warped version of reality.

As a leader, what you need to do is to reinforce the link between the old and the new, how the foundation of the future has been built upon the work of the past, to show how one will flow into the other. You cannot bypass this phase and you cannot predict how people will respond. But you know there will be a range of reactions.

Beginnings

THE CHANGE MODEL

- Beginnings happen once people see change as gain.
- Beginnings do not occur until individuals have aligned themselves with a new vision and purpose.
- People have to embrace the change before beginnings can occur.

Adapted from William Bridges, <u>Managing Transitions.</u> Cambridge, MA, DaCapo Press, 1991, 2003

The expected positive impacts of any change will come to fruition only when the majority of the team begins to see the change as a gain rather than loss. They must intellectually and emotionally align themselves with the new vision and purpose that the changes are intended to create. Although the change process can be hard on people, we hope that the new approaches, systems or models will be appreciated for their potential value and benefit. If this value can be perceived, members of the organization can rebuild their trust in whatever new scenario is unfolding and operate with a sense of trust and commitment.

One key problem in any change scenario is often referred to as organizational misalignment. This refers to the fact that upper management usually gets to the beginnings phase more quickly than the rest of the organization. This is because they are involved in rolling out changes or could have had a hand in their design. That level of control accelerates their comfort with the change well ahead of the rest of their team. It is very important that leaders do not demonstrate frustration or impatience at the pace of adaptation to the change.

Anyone who has been through organizational change knows that change is difficult. Part of the reason for that is that people are complex and it is difficult to predict how any individual will react to things. I worked for a fellow one time who actually became a perfect barometer for what to expect from employee reactions to change because it turned out his initial inclination was wrong almost 100 percent of the time. If he thought somebody would take things in stride, they would get belligerent. If we were worried about somebody melting down, they seemed to handle it well.

So the bottom line is we have to figure out what we want to do to help everyone move through the change process. In the simplest terms, what you need to do is show two critical things: concern and connections.

Concern: Anticipate concerns. By using Bridges' change model, you can be better prepared to recognize the reaction of members of your team to various announcements, process adjustments, people moves and other changes. By alerting yourself to look for understandable reactions in others, you can consider how to craft your response.

Demonstrate empathy. Empathy is putting yourself in someone else's shoes and seeing things from their perspective. By being able to anticipate some reactions, you can discuss things in a more empathic manner. For instance, simply stating that the uncertainty of the situation is probably troubling for everybody, including yourself, makes it more legitimate for everyone to discuss it.

Connections: Help people stay connected to the new vision. Part of your job as a leader is to link the old and the new. When you can conclusively do so, reinforce how each person's contributions will fit into the new vision. In times of heightened anxiety, be careful about making casual promises just to calm people down. Be prepared and get comfortable with saying "I don't know."

Make opportunities to be involved in the process. When you are going through change, it's the perfect time to rethink systems, processes and even organizational structure. Get your team involved in providing input. If they have more ownership of what will happen, they will feel less like victims.

Communicate Consistently

As you move through any change process, always be prepared to communicate the four P's:

- Purpose: Why are we doing this?
- Picture: What's the big picture?
- Plan: You do have a plan for us, don't you?
- Parts: Are there parts for us all? Can we all be involved?

Leading a team through any organizational change is a great learning experience but it requires constant vigilance to ensure that the intended outcomes or improvements from any changes will actually come to fruition. It takes a great plan and the constant updating of that plan, and one critical part of that plan is your communication strategy.

FIVE MYTHS ABOUT CHANGING BEHAVIOR

To exist is to change, to change is to mature,
to mature is to go on creating oneself endlessly.
—HENRI BERGSON, FRENCH PHILOSOPHER

I HAVE FOLLOWED *Fast Company* magazine for many years. In 2005, the cover feature of its May issue was "Change or Die," by Alan Deutschman.[32] That title caught my attention because change is one of the key things I discuss with my clients. Here are the five myths about changing behavior that were discussed in that article and some ideas I have about what you can do to learn about changing your behavior going forward.

Myth One: Crisis is a powerful impetus for change.

You would think that a major health crisis would be an excellent reason to rethink your lifestyle choices to ensure that such a calamity could be prevented in the future. Deutschman's article notes that people who have open heart surgery often revert to some of the same behaviors that created the crisis. In fact, studies by Dr. Edward Miller, the dean of the medical school and CEO of the hospital at Johns Hopkins University, indicated that an astonishing 90 percent of people went back to the same behavior that created their problem once they had recuperated from surgery. The fact that smoking, drinking, poor diet, lack of exercise or using drugs may have created the need for surgery did not prevent the resumption of the bad habits! People endured the surgery—the crisis—but never seemed to connect the dots about how their behavior caused the crisis. "Denial is not just a river in Egypt," as the saying goes.

Myth Two: Fear is a great motivator for change.

You'd think that fear of dying would be a great motivator for change, but as we saw in the previous example, that didn't work for 90 percent of the people who had open heart surgery. The idea that fear of a particular outcome, such as loss of your job, demotion, a decrease in pay or other potential motivators that may cause you to adjust your behavior, does seem to make sense. But the reality is that fear of a negative outcome has only a short-term effect, and fear tends to diminish over time, allowing old habits and behaviors to reemerge.

Myth Three: The facts will set us free.

Difficult changes are often caused by new and challenging realities, like getting a new boss, a decline in markets or changes in customer tastes. New realities do cause a need for adjustments, but this also suggests that the intellectual realities will trump the emotional or psychological reactions we have to new situations. The opposite is true. We have made connections with the things we have gotten used to and know well. We may understand that things are changing, but letting go is very difficult because of our connections to people, familiar settings and work or because of the fear of the unknown that awaits us. We can become emotionally frozen to the current state of things. It takes time and a concerted effort to reassert the need for change by the change leaders.

Myth Four: Small, gradual changes are always easier to make and sustain.

This myth is intellectually appealing because it argues for an incremental approach where success along the way reinforces itself. But the reality is that for every step forward with gradual changes, there is the risk of another half-step backward toward the old and familiar. We tend to see gradual changes as an opportunity to hold on to the way things had been done before. The other school of thought is often referred to as the "rip the Band-Aid off" approach, which is probably more painful in the short run but can both accelerate and reinforce the new state of things and put more distance between the old and the new.

Myth Five: We can't change because our brains have been "hardwired" early in life.

I am well aware of my age bias on this issue and do believe it is true that the older you get the more comfortable you become in performing tasks in ways that are more familiar to you. The benefits of pattern recognition allow us to productively manage through a barrage of tasks and challenges, but you can get "stuck" in old patterns. I believe with the proper understanding of the need for change and incentives to do so, people at any age can embrace change and progress. And I am confident that people have an infinite capacity to continue to learn. The ability of organizations to create opportunities to blend the old with the new, using the experience of its seasoned staff to collaborate with the developing leaders of tomorrow, requires that many stereotypes be turned on their heads.

Ask yourself:

- What motivates me to make changes? A crisis or opportunities for growth?

- Which of these myths seems to affect me the most as I reflect on recent changes I have worked through?

- As I reflect on recent changes I have worked through, what helped me adapt quickly and effectively? (Warning: This can be tough to discern!)

FIVE COMMON MISCONCEPTIONS ABOUT CHANGE— AND WHAT YOU CAN DO ABOUT THEM

If you want to make enemies, try to change something.
—WOODROW WILSON

CHANGE IS CHALLENGING, both personally and professionally. In Europe and North America, almost 50 percent of marriages end in divorce. A marriage involves only two people. Making change happen in your own company, even if it's for sound business reasons, has an even gloomier outlook.

According to Gregory P. Shea, Ph.D., and Cassie Solomon, co-authors of *Leading Successful Change: 8 Keys to Making Change Work*, "Leading a major change effort in any organization, let alone a large and complex one, presents a first order challenge, often among the most difficult of any executive career. In fact, the numbers show that up to 75 percent of change efforts fail."[33]

When you add in the complexities of company culture, language and country or continental differences, the news is even bleaker, Shea and Solomon say. "But the risk of failure gets even worse—and more expensive—when it comes to mergers and acquisitions. More recently, a 2007 study by Hay Group and the Sorbonne found that more than 90 percent of mergers in Europe fail to reach financial goals."

Now let's be clear, no one of good conscience approaches change with anything but the best intentions, and usually there are high expectations for financial efficiencies as well as marketing and operational synergies. But many change initiatives, despite good intentions, unravel. Here are five misconceptions about change and at least one antidote to each.

Misconception One: Change happens quickly once announced.

Senior managers and change leaders expect that once the official announcement has taken place, people will rally around the obvious benefits of change and begin to adapt to the new structures, reporting relationships and business realignments. But personal relationships, familiarity and comfort with current coworkers and processes and fear of the unknown create a visceral inertia. And no two employees can be expected to react the same.

Leaders need to have a long-range plan that mirrors the expected improvements that were the basis for the change in the first place. Manage the change like you would any process improvement and have prearranged targets for checking in on progress along the way. Start with the beginning in mind to determine how you will measure the effectiveness of not only progress along the way but how the ultimate results match up with the initial intentions.

Misconception Two: Change usually begins with a definitive event.

In my most recent corporate home, we completed a merger with our European partner that was based in England. The corporate head of human resources, who was English, hired the head of a Welsh theater company, who had worked for John Cleese of "Monty Python" fame, to create a three-act play that compared and made light of American versus English culture, primarily focusing on the differences between baseball and cricket. It was very balanced and very clever. We put this on in the United Kingdom and in three locations in the United States, creating a video for our international team. This was referred to as the "launch" of the new, combined company. It was great fun to experience and enormously expensive to produce. But it didn't help a bit in overcoming resistance to change on an individual, team or organizational level.

Leaders need to be creative and insightful in creating an impetus for change, and a memorable event or two along the way certainly can be interesting and provoke dialogue about the change. But do not let pomp trump circumstance.

Misconception Three: Time takes care of everything.

It would be very convenient if, as time passed, the raw feelings and grievances, real or imagined, just faded away. But the reality is some people have such a difficult time with change that they refuse to let go of the "good old days." The reality is that some employees, especially those who legitimately had a great deal of ownership in what had been developed in the past, do have logical reasons for having a hard time letting go. If leadership fails to acknowledge the contributions of those along the way or actually denigrates them in some manner, it will only lengthen the transition process.

Leaders need to be able to drive change down to the lowest level possible in an organization. You must say goodbye to the past in a respectful manner because no matter how radical a shift you may be taking, the past was prologue to the present. Reinforce its foundational importance.

Misconception Four: Everyone who is not on board with the changes has something wrong with them.

You cannot expect large groups to adapt to change in a lockstep fashion; people progress at different rates and there's nothing wrong with that. In the short run, change can often be challenging for those learning new processes and routines. It can also be difficult for customers to adapt and that creates a host of additional challenges for those who work most closely with these customers.

Leaders need to listen to suggestions along the way to continually improve on all new processes. They cannot allow themselves to abandon new approaches because of naysayers, but how they accommodate new ideas along the way can assuage many concerns of both employees and customers.

Misconception Five: If the communication is done right the first time, that's enough.

A great deal of effort and forethought must be put into the process of communicating the new reality efficiently and effectively. But even more important, everyone needs to be apprised of the progress along the way and the milestones that point to normalizing around a new way of doing business. You must look at the pipeline of communication that needs to be developed and consistently delivered over a multiyear process.

Leaders should follow this advice from Winston Churchill: "If you have an important point to make, don't try to be subtle or clever. Use the pile driver. Hit the point once. Then come back and hit it again. Then hit it a third time, a tremendous whack."

Ask yourself:

- What is the purpose of this internal change or structural shift (merger, acquisition, or realignment)? How and when shall we measure its success?

- Do I have a transition team in place that is charged with implementing, measuring and tracking progress for all to see?

- Am I committed to a communications plan that is consistent, transparent and compelling?

Why Things Often Get Worse Before They Get Better

Never, never, never, never give up!
—Winston Churchill

Golf is a sport that requires a lot of practice to create the muscle memory to consistently hit the ball well. It has taken me many years to learn to play well enough to enjoy the game and not embarrass myself. It's now a passion and I have had the good fortune of playing many fine courses with lots of great people. Golf brings to mind two critical questions I have for any leader:

1. Do you solicit the right feedback to ensure that you continue to improve your leadership effectiveness and the results that you, your team and your organization demand?
2. How often have you tried to incorporate new skills, tools or habits at work only to fall back on older habits because the changes became too difficult?

To help you understand why we often abandon well-intentioned changes, I will use two parallel examples. The first will deal with golf, but I promise you that I'll keep that short and sweet. The second will be all about how you can delegate tasks more efficiently and effectively. I will also share with you a model showing how the difficulty of making changes affects us and why persistence usually pays off.

Determining What's Wrong

The first step is always the hardest step. It is trying to figure out what the problem is and what the potential solutions might be. One common golf challenge for right-handers like me is what we call a slice. This is when the ball gets pushed to the right instead of going straight. Severe slices can take us out of bounds and moderate ones can leave us in the taller grass, making those shots more difficult. The causes for slicing the ball have to do with how you address the ball, how you grip the club and various other things. Hitting a golf ball looks easy, but minor problems add up to lots of extra strokes during a round.

One critical leadership challenge that my clients consistently face is how to delegate effectively. They often find they have too much work to do themselves and need to take something off their plate. The need for delegating is clear but it requires planning to do well, especially when you first embrace the concept.

The need to adjust your approach to hitting a golf ball or to reducing the feelings of being overwhelmed by all the work that confronts you is obvious. Each problem has a potential range of solutions, but you must select the appropriate ones and implement them. A lesson from a golf pro and hitting a lot of range balls can help you with your slice. The delegation issue is more complicated, but it, too, can become easier once you address the issue instead of ignoring it.

Choosing a New Way or Habit

Although we understand what it feels like to be overwhelmed by too much work, we often fail to understand what the causes are. It becomes difficult to consider delegation when we consistently procrastinate about attacking issues and investing the time needed to plan for how we can tackle them. Some repetitive tasks and challenges don't require much planning, since we know what to do and just have to do it. When there are newer or more difficult challenges, we often have to look for different solutions. Leaders resist delegating for several reasons:

- They fear that if they are not involved in all discussions they will lose control.

- They believe they have to be infinitely available to participate in all meetings and conference calls as well keep up with an avalanche of email.
- They don't know how to use their staff well by delegating the right things to the right people.
- They don't understand how to set expectations about what feedback they need about the progress of various tasks along the way.

If the leader comes to grips with these issues and plans for effectively delegating to members of his or her team, then, just like the cure for the slice, the situation should begin to improve immediately, right? Unfortunately, no. This chart will show you why:

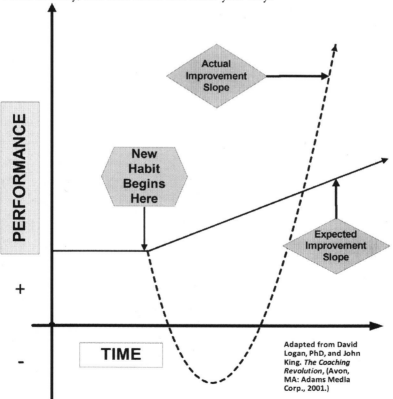

Adapted from David Logan, PhD, and John King. *The Coaching Revolution*, (Avon, MA: Adams Media Corp., 2001.)

When we adjust a current behavior or begin to institute a new habit, we are full of the joys of spring about the potential results. Think New Year's resolutions and diets. It happens to us all. We expect that things will improve and the slope of the improvement will continue to climb right up. But reality intrudes! When we make behavioral changes, we run into resistance. In golf, when you have an important shot to hit and you begin thinking about all the changes in your swing that are needed to overcome your slice problem, you will often revert to old habits out of comfort or forgetfulness. Bad outcomes can certainly encourage us to go back and practice more. So in the short run, we can discover that our performance gets a little worse until the change becomes the "new normal" and we commit to it without thinking about it. Then we see that the slope of the improvement part of the graph is much greater than it would have been.

I have seen the challenge of delegation with many clients over the years. The reasons for resisting that I listed are very real and very difficult to overcome. If you fail to inform subordinates about certain information they will need to carry out delegated tasks, you may end up with resistance or anger on the part of the subordinates. Planning for delegation takes time. That's why you often hear it's easier and quicker for someone to just do it themselves. But their time crunch never lessens and their staff don't get the chance to grow and develop as they could. So the give-and-take that's needed to shape a leader into being an effective delegator literally does create its own time crunch, enhancing the decline in the slope of the improvement line in the short run.

These challenges in implementing new habits or behaviors often cause us to abandon well laid plans and intentions. Again, think of diets. If you have the patience and determination to stick to your plan and adjust as needed, you will begin to see the evidence of the improvements that you seek. Leaders who delegate more find they have more time for their own work, and not only does the work get done but there are new opportunities for growth and development on the part of the staff that takes on the delegated duties.

I wish I could say that my efforts at building a better swing by implementing more effective habits in my golf game have made me into the golfer I desire to be. But I can't. But as I like to say to my financial advisor as we discuss investment options, "Hope is not a strategy." You have to be persistent in overcoming the discomfort that changes are creating for you and recognize incremental progress along the way.

I don't mean to say that you shouldn't abandon certain behavioral or process modifications that don't seem to work, but I believe if you can better understand the very predictable challenges of implementing any change before you really see the return on the investment longer-term, you can find the persistence that you need to stay the course and implement your plan.

To make any change or habit a reality, ask yourself:

- How will I take time to plan? What do I want to do and how will that be different?

- How will I tell others what I am doing and why and enlist their support?

- What milestones can I develop for charting progress?

- When I've successfully implemented the change or habit, will I take the time to step back and reflect on how I did it so I can learn from my success?

What Exactly Are You Changing— and Why?

"Few things are more striking than the fact that while the best are nearly powerless to effect change, the worst are so potent."
—George F. Watts

A client who is a successful financial advisor once shared with me an interesting phrase and mentioned it was used by a CEO she knew when things got bogged down in his company: "Something is causing nothing to happen." I'd like to briefly explore the implications of this powerful insight in relation to how high-performing companies handle change.

In "The Three Questions,"[34] William Bridges, Ph.D., has written extensively about today's frequent and disruptive changes, stating that there are three key questions that need to be asked when change occurs:

- What is changing?
- What will actually be different because of the change?
- Who's going to lose what?

In business, the success of a change effort can be directly correlated to the level of candor and thoroughness engaged in the analysis of these questions. Take, for example, the leader of a national sales force responsible for almost $500 million in revenues, who recently decided to adjust the compensation plan for the advisors. This change was meant to increase revenues for the firm, encourage certain behaviors from the advisors and be fair to the clients. So the constituents were the firm, the advisors and clients. There will always be certain levels of resistance to any change, but in this case, here are some the answers to the three questions for this change in sales compensation:

- What is changing?

This was made very clear to all: Fees on certain transactions were going to increase after several years of holding them steady. Plenty of "what if" scenarios were played out, and before changes were announced, a huge amount of analysis was done. What had happened that increased the costs to the firm? Were additional benefits going to accrue to the clients? What was the competition doing?

- What will actually be different because of the change?

This answer was more complex because different advisors operated under different investment models and the impact on each varied. What would be different in the plan was very clear, but the leaders allotted time for advisors and teams to absorb how the new policy would affect them and their clients, given the intricacies of the different investment models. Again, various "what if" scenarios were played out with the effects on all constituencies.

- Who's going to lose what?

Just adjusting to a changed model can be considered a loss for many because it requires them to adapt to new things. Often this concern is avoided and not discussed because it's uncomfortable, but until people can see a change as a gain, they will resist. In this case, the losses were that some clients would have to pay more for some services/ advice and the advisors would have to inform or "sell" the increase to their clients. Some advisors would also make a little less on some transactions but more on others. It would require some advisors to rethink elements of their business model. Unfortunately, some people will focus on potential losses, however remote, tiny or even nonexistent until the benefits come into view.

By taking great care to not only anticipate and plan for this change but also manage the communication process well, this company was able to implement their changes with minimal pushback. The potential losses were all held up to the light of day and dealt with. The anticipated benefits have occurred for the firm and the advisors, without any major resistance by the clients.

When you, as a leader, feel like nothing is happening or that the change is evolving in slower or even unanticipated ways, use the three questions suggested by Bridges to help you analyze what the something may be that's causing it. It's an excellent diagnostic tool.

Ask yourself:

- When I prepare to announce the changes, have I considered how to honor all the hard work that got us to where we are today?

- Have I thought through the impacts of this change on everyone so I can anticipate how to communicate the impacts empathically?

- Can I target my persuasion appropriately to respond to whomever might feel they are "losing" the most from this change?

MANAGING CHANGE FOR YOUR
NUMBER ONE CLIENT—YOU!

The world hates change, yet it is the only thing that has brought progress.
—CHARLES KETTERING

THE PACE OF CHANGE in today's world is truly staggering. The Austrian economist Joseph Schumpeter referred to the impact of such disruptive change as "creative destruction." Catchy phrase, until you have to deal with those effects in your own life. Today, disruptive change occurs globally, and no industry or business is immune.

According to "Bend It, Change It, Dunk It: Graphene," an article in *The New York Times*, April 13, 2014 by Nick Bilton, a new material called graphene is "the strongest, thinnest material known to exist. A form of carbon, it can conduct electricity and heat better than anything else. And get ready for this: It is not only the hardest material in the world, but also one of the most pliable. Only a single atom thick, it has been called the wonder material. Graphene could change the electronics industry, ushering in flexible devices, supercharged quantum computers, electronic clothing and computers that can interface with the cells in your body."

The potential positive effects of this wonderful new discovery eventually could create significant advantages in everyone's lives. Although great opportunities abound, graphene may have an incredibly disruptive effect on many industries—and on the people who work in them—that are currently using other materials. So what does this have to do with change and its effect on you? The answer is plenty, and in this chapter I'd like to explore:

1. How change affects us emotionally and psychologically and

2. How to work through the inevitable changes that will affect our jobs and lives.

The changes we endure in the workplace are varied. Mergers, acquisitions, divestitures, closings, reorganizations, new systems and new bosses are but a few of them, and I have experienced them all in my career. Each poses unique challenges, but there are common themes that should resonate with us all.

When changes are announced, we all go through our own personal calculations about how the proposed changes will affect us. What will the new boss be like and how will he or she view my skills and style? Will the new operating system take advantage of my previous knowledge or will I have to face a challenging learning curve that puts me at risk? In a merger or acquisition, are there duplicate roles that make me potentially redundant? If I have had my head down doing my job and living my life while neglecting the need to network, how do I start reconnecting?

Although you may intellectually understand the need for new systems, the rationale for a merger or why you were passed over for a promotion in favor of someone with more relevant experience, emotionally you can get "stuck" in dealing with these issues. Our initial reaction to many changes is that we expect that the impact on us will be negative—a loss. The key challenge is that there is so much unknown about many changes until they develop further. We may not be able to count on much initial clarity.

In his groundbreaking book on change, *Managing Transitions: Making the Most of Change,*[35] William Bridges looks at change in three stages:
- Endings: Letting Go of the Old
- Neutral Zone: The Wilderness as the New Reality Develops
- The New Beginning

In the Endings phase, our concerns about how change will affect us—our losses—really weigh on us. It is important in this stage to:

- Gather as much information about what's going on as possible. Attend informational meetings. Read whatever you can. Ask your leadership about what they expect or know. Accept the answer "I don't know" because it will often be true at that time.
- Maintain as positive an attitude as possible. As Yoda said to Luke Skywalker, "Don't give in to the Dark Side." During the "endings" phase, catastrophic fantasies—worst case scenarios about what may or may not happen that are not grounded in any reality—can flourish. Sometimes this is a little like gallows humor, and I would encourage you to avoid it. It can become a feeding frenzy among coworkers and it is unhealthy.
- Review your accomplishments and contributions to the organization. We often are so busy we fail to take stock of all we have done. This is necessary and healthy.
- Reenergize your networking efforts. We often fail to invest any time here, mostly because we are too busy or don't know how. Develop a list of your top 30 contacts and begin to reach out to see what's going on in their worlds and in the job market. Do not approach this as looking for jobs, as that is the wrong way to relaunch networking efforts.
- Don't let up on your current duties. It does not make sense to throttle back on your work now, since it reflects your most current contributions. You may be fighting a malaise with your own energy or enthusiasm or with your coworkers or team, but strive for accomplishing whatever you can.

The Neutral Zone, or Wilderness, can be difficult because things are on hold and that is very unnerving. We would all like to get things over and move on, but given the complexity of many organizations, that is often not a reality. Bridges acknowledges that there are three feelings that emerge during the Neutral Phase: uncertainty, mistrust and self-preservation. In business we often resist discussing the impact of feelings because it can get messy. It reminds me of Tom Hanks' admonition to one of his female baseball players in "A League of Their Own," "There's no crying in baseball!" But we ignore these at our peril:

• **Uncertainty:** The challenge of change is that it is not a linear or completely logical process. A client of mine likes to say he hires employees but human beings always seem to show up. People react differently to the uncertainty of change. Someone once said some people prefer the certainty of misery to the misery of uncertainty. You've heard people who complain about their jobs. Their boss is an idiot, their coworkers are dunces, the pay and benefits are awful and the commute is a real bear. So you ask them why they don't look for a new job and their response is, "Well, it's a steady gig and I've been there a long time." We can never really understand the depths of how individuals react to the uncertainty of a situation and how it may affect them. The issue is always about how you control what you can control. Reinforce what you can and accept what you cannot.

• **Mistrust:** Because the situation is changing, many of the things that you counted on before are in flux. This may reduce the trust level you have for the organization, the leadership and even your boss. If you relied on certain promises or expectations, trust can be difficult. Try to separate the organizational needs from your personal situation.

• **Self-Preservation:** In times of change, we often are asked to "take one for the team" and move beyond the personal impact of any change. My response to that is always, "Hogwash!" You have every right to be concerned about the effects of change on yourself, your career and your family. No one is ever going to take care of you better than yourself. You just want to be sure that others don't get the impression that it is only you that you are worried about because that level of self-focus and selfishness can have an impact on your reputation going forward.

In any change situation that can have significant impact on your career, Bridges suggests you always ask yourself four key questions:

1. **Purpose:** Why are we doing this?

2. **Picture:** What's the big picture here? How does this fit in to what's happening in the industry and the global marketplace, and how does it exploit the organizational strengths we have?

3. **Plan:** Does the organization have a plan for us or are they making it up as they go along? Seek as much information as you can to understand that.

4. **Parts:** What's my part and how can I be involved?

I encourage everyone to redouble their efforts in building relationships and their network of connections on an ongoing basis. This is helpful for you, your career and your value to any organization in the long term. Make this a priority going forward.

Change is always going to be difficult. Keep in mind these inspiring words from that great philosopher, Woody Allen, "It's not that I'm afraid of death. It's just that I don't want to be there when it happens." Prepare yourself for change and you can enjoy the ride no matter how bumpy it may be.

Ask yourself:

- No matter how radical the change, have I considered how I will honor the past contributions that helped get me where I am today?

- Have I thought about the four Ps and can I clearly articulate the purpose, picture, plan and parts as succinctly and completely as possible?

- Have I acknowledged that people want to know how change affects them and do I have a solid timeline for telling them as much as I can as quickly as possible?

RELATIONSHIPS

INTRO: Relationships—
The Key to Connecting and Getting a Voice for Your Vision

In preparing this introduction, I was thinking about how relationship management has been important to me in my career. I've actually been selling directly for about 22 years of my 30-plus year career. I managed a wholesale distribution operation across three states, and I've been selling my talents the entire time I've been in the coaching business. A salesman obviously is not going to generate any sales unless he or she is able to find customers. Any salesperson will tell you that a buyer's decisions are often significantly based on the quality of the relationship between the buyer and seller. The only way to ensure that a relationship develops effectively is through a consistent effort by the seller to create a connection that is productive for both parties.

When I think of my time in the corporate world as an internal practitioner, I realize that I was always selling there as well. If I wanted to implement a new program or process, or change existing ones, I needed to sell the ideas to my constituents, the leaders and managers in the organization that I served. I must admit that I did not readily embrace the sales part of my internal role, primarily because I lacked a lot of confidence in how to manage an effective relationship like that. I got along with people just fine, but my influence in any organization was often based on my positional power and the support of the senior leadership in approving various initiatives. But it was selling nonetheless.

One job I held in the corporate world was manager of sales compensation for a sales force that operated throughout North and South America. I managed 28 sales plans for the variety of selling channels the organization had. I was always impressed with the way these men and women were able to maintain our sales position as the number one firm in our industry. When I ran a wholesale distribution operation, I sponsored a trip to Hawaii for my customers who met their sales goals. The customers were motivated by the trip as well as the sales and profits that came from meeting their goals. But it was my salesmen and I who made these relationships work, and we did that by our consistent connections and the trust we developed with our customers.

In my coaching experience, I have dealt with leaders of investment banks, private equity groups, wealth management groups and senior legal partners. The one thing in common among all these high-performing leaders was their focus on knowing their customers and managing those important relationships. These people not only know what's currently happening in whatever industry they follow, but they are generally attuned to specific business sectors that they come to know in depth. The most critical element of these individual successes is the ability to have the connections that make the leaders of these companies repeatedly call on them for their services. Many seem to have a science in how they maintain their visibility in connection with these industry leaders. There's actually a whole industry, led by ACT and Salesforce.com, whose focus is managing the connections between sellers and potential buyers or current customers. But it all boils down to the quality of the relationships that are established and nurtured over time.

One of the best models I use with my coaching clients comes from the work of Peter Block and is reviewed in some detail in the chapter "Allies Versus Adversaries: A Framework for Discussing Relationships." On the next page is the key relationship model from that chapter.

In short, this model contrasts the levels of trust and agreement we have with various individuals. On the right hand side of the model, you have allies and opponents. With an ally you have high trust and

Allies vs. Adversaries

From: Peter Block, *The Empowered Manager*, San Francisco, CA
Josey-Bass Publishers, 1987, page 139

high agreement. With an opponent, you have high trust but low agreement. We cannot expect to have agreement on all things with those we trust. We need to be able to disagree in an agreeable fashion, but in those conversations the focus is on learning more from each other about different perspectives and ideas that we hope enhance or improve the quality of the idea or initiative being contemplated. To state it another way, an opponent will beat up your idea, not you, because of the trust that exists.

The only way to confirm agreement or disagreement is to spend the time to lay out your idea or suggestion and patiently take in the feedback and insights with the person you are sharing this with. Making the time to engage in these conversations is difficult to do based on the pressures of the current work world and, perversely enough, the ubiquitous communication tools we have to share information. Sherry Turkle has written extensively about the technology of mobile connections and the impact it has on one-on-one communication. In her *New York Times* opinion article on April 12, 2012, "The Flight from Conversation," she says, "We've become accustomed to a new way of being 'alone together.' Technology enabled, we are able to be with one another, and also elsewhere, connected to wherever we want to be."

How often have you been in meetings where, except for the one who is speaking and maybe the individual being addressed, everyone else is busily tapping away on their smart phone or laptop, catching up on their email or other connections? It saddens me to see an attractive couple in a restaurant with their noses buried in their smartphones and no dialogue between them. I have seen effective leaders whose job is to find and execute transactions for their organizations. You can't build a connection without conversations, and yet in the incredibly harried and busy world that most of us work in, there not only seems to be little time for conversations but also less interest in them. People simply prefer the control they have over sending out emails or texts to the actual give-and-take of a conversation or spirited argument.

Because we've let our communication and dialogue skills atrophy—assuming they were reasonably well developed in the first place—we must become critically focused on purposefully developing and cultivating trusting relationships. This focus is a key to organizational success. In addition, your value in an organization is directly affected by the variety and quality of your internal and external relationships. Internally, knowing who to call to gain support for your efforts or to garner "intelligence" about different perspectives and plans, will always be advantageous.

Years ago, most organizations had internal functions (like the travel department, training and even security) that have now been outsourced in the interest of focus on that company's "core competencies." This trend gained momentum in the 1980s, and today organizations actively manage support from a variety of specialist companies that have developed deep knowledge and experience. So individuals' networks of connections must extend well beyond the company that gives them their paycheck to stay current in their field. Maintaining a broad network enhances their value within their organization.

This chart illustrates that leaders and managers in a company need to have awareness and connection with academic and industry thought leaders, consultants and highly qualified outsourced service vendors. Every leader does not need deep resources in all areas, but staying abreast of current trends requires that you actively manage your external relationships.

THE COMPANY – Today

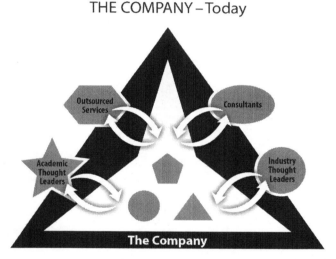

Given the incredible time pressures in the working world today, it isn't easy to spend some of your precious time building relationships. But I assure you that the leaders I admire most are focused on the quality of the relationships they have with their teams, within their organization and externally. The chapters in this section focus on improving relationships, and I hope you find ideas that will resonate with you and serve you well.

Trust men and they will be true to you;
treat them greatly and they will show themselves great.
—Ralph Waldo Emerson

ALLIES VERSUS ADVERSARIES:
A FRAMEWORK FOR DISCUSSING RELATIONSHIPS

To effectively communicate, we must realize that we are
all different in the way we perceive the world and use this
understanding as a guide to our communication with others.
—TONY ROBBINS

HAVE YOU EVER BEEN a little stumped when someone asked how you would describe your relationship with a coworker? Developing and maintaining strong relationships is a key part of organizational success.

I had a client who struggled to summarize how she felt about a colleague. She admired his experience, work ethic, creativity and communication skills but didn't feel confident about the nature of her connection with him. He displayed some good leadership traits, but there were things about the relationship that made her cautious and uncomfortable in her dealings with him. So I asked her:

When you disagree with him:

- Does he stay focused on getting the best solution or is it about his solution?
- Does he take things personally when the conversation should just be business?
- Does he demonstrate a sincere interest in your perspectives?

How you manage agreements and disagreements is critical to your success. Do you feel he:

- Is reliable and dependable in doing what he says when he says he will?
- Gives you honest and candid feedback in a constructive manner when you ask for it?
- Will maintain a confidence you shared with him?

If you answered yes for all three of these questions, you can be sure you are well on your way to a trusting relationship.

Peter Block wrote an insightful book, *The Empowered Manager: Positive Political Skills at Work,*[36] and in Chapter 5, "Building Support for Your Vision: Negotiating with Allies and Adversaries," he creates a model that can assist you in dealing with these potentially competing demands of trust and agreement. A few basics to consider:

Trust: Trust takes time to develop and nurture and can be lost in a flash. You need to be consistent, assertive and politically adept at building a coalition to support your vision or goal. But positive political skills end when you act duplicitously. The three questions above about reliability, honest feedback and maintaining confidences are good guidelines for behavior that looks trustworthy to others. You must work diligently on maintaining trust.

Agreement: You can never expect blanket agreement from others. Those who profess to provide that are "yes" people and can be more dangerous than a cantankerous, "prove it to me" type because they want to agree more than exercise deliberate judgment. What matters most is how people agree to disagree. This will become clearer as you examine the model Block created on the next page.

Let's examine each of the five positions on this chart:

Allies: High Trust/High Agreement: They share your vision or goals and want to achieve outcomes by behaving in a manner consistent with yours.

Allies vs. Adversaries

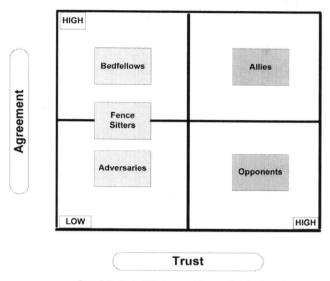

From: Peter Block, *The Empowered Manager*, San Francisco, CA
Josey-Bass Publishers, 1987, page 139

Adversaries: Low Trust/Low Agreement: People fall into this quadrant because you have failed to negotiate agreement or build trust with them. Maybe you have tried, but they won't cooperate or have a radically different vision. If you confirm your boss is an adversary, be prepared to move on. If a subordinate is an adversary, the best thing you can do is help them to move on.

Bedfellows: High Agreement/Low Trust: They profess agreement with you on many topics, but you do not believe you have a trusting relationship. There seems to be a lot of caution about their connection with you or with their voicing candid opinions about your vision.

Fence Sitters: Low Trust/Unknown Agreement: These are often the ultimate bureaucrats and operate out of pessimism and helplessness. They may be glib and seemingly effective communicators, but they consistently lie about their positions. You have to try to flush them out to establish their position, but these relationships are often not worth much effort.

Opponents: High Trust/Low Agreement: These are folks you trust but who often disagree. "Opponent" is an accurate but unfortunate term, since our society teaches us to vanquish our opponents. You need to carefully cultivate opponents because they will beat up your ideas but not you. That will usually mean that you end up with better ideas!

Use this model to reflect on your current relationships. With each person, for each task or initiative that comes up, you must exchange vision, purpose or goals; affirm or negotiate agreement; and affirm or reaffirm and negotiate trust.

Ask yourself:

- Do I reach out periodically to affirm the quality of the relationships with my allies and adversaries?

- Can I think of a colleague I was able to build trust with over time? How can I repeat that as needed with others?

- How agreeable am I to disagree with? Do I defend my position at all costs or do I really look for the best solutions, which could be someone else's suggestions or a compromise of our ideas?

Three Trust Busters
and How to Improve
Employee Engagement

Trust is the glue of life. It's the most essential ingredient in effective communication. It's the foundational principle that holds all relationships.
—Stephen Covey

At a family wedding I attended, I spoke with a few young people who have three things in common:

- They are gainfully employed college graduates.
- Most are off their parents' payrolls.
- They feel disengaged and disappointed in their current work situations, and they all work for well-known, reputable firms.

I was happy to hear about the first two facts and concerned about the third issue because it affects so many people. I have three children of my own in their 20s and these are common complaints from them as well. Disengagement is prevalent in the workforce and employers should be concerned. A simple strategy for building trust can go a long way toward alleviating employee disengagement.

Bruce Tulgan, the founder of Rainmaker Thinking, has written extensively about trends in the workplace, especially focusing on the intergenerational differences in challenges that exist. In "Pent-Up Departure Demand: The Swelling Ranks of Employees Who Would Leave if They Could," (*Just Thinking* newsletter, March 14, 2014),[37] he shares some key results from extensive survey work he has done over the last five years.

Tulgan's firm analyzed data trends from 41,238 respondents from January 2009 to January 2014. They were able to track 2,874 respondents consistently over this five-year period. The startling finding was that more than 46 percent of employees in the civilian workforce have felt "stuck," meaning they had an unfulfilled desire to leave their current job for at least a year. Nearly 25 percent of employees said they had felt stuck for more than three years. This pent up departure desire is equally distributed among high performers and average performers and is lowest among low performers.

Many employees who feel stuck have substantial levels of dissatisfaction, and more than 90 percent of them self-report diminished performance in one or more of the following areas: commitment, effort, morale, willingness to go the extra mile and eagerness to contribute their best ideas. Many of these employees have seen their companies tighten their belts in this challenging economy and are often faced with poor pay and benefits, burdensome schedules, added work without additional compensation and a workplace not conducive to effective collaboration.

These individuals do not get enough support or don't like their immediate managers. This latter concern is the most common issue for the 20-somethings I was conversing with at that wedding. They describe their immediate managers as overwhelmed, unfocused, unresponsive to their suggestions and, in general, poor leaders.

The largest dissatisfaction of the young people I spoke with was that their ideas and suggestions were not taken seriously or their managers showed a fundamental distrust of their ability to make valuable contributions.

These young people had a systematic process of looking at the flow of work they were engaged in. They were not just whining about things in their jobs. They saw great opportunities for improving what was going on and believed they were consistently ignored or not taken seriously.

One criticism I have heard about the millennial generation is that they expect immediate results and immediate rewards for their suggestions. This was not the tone of the discussions that I had.

As I thought about my conversations with these young employees, two themes came through loud and clear:

1. The leaders of these young people sounded not only overwhelmed but incapable of sifting through potentially valuable suggestions productively. I attribute this problem to the frenetic pace of most leaders as well as to their lack of training and development.
2. Many of the responses of leaders to the suggestions of their youthful cohorts reflected an attitude that screams, "I don't trust you."

If you're a leader, especially if you want to improve engagement of employees in the younger generations, you must be careful not to be seen as a "trust buster." Here are some ways to overcome your entrenched attitudes and open up more to engage employees:

1. Either/Or: The listener presses for closure and the listening style reflects a black or white view of the situation; it's either this way or it's that way. When there's no allowing for any gray area, which could be a compromise or a synthesis of a couple of ideas, people with different ideas feel that their contributions are automatically shut down. Our polarized political situation in the United States reflects just such a perspective. The very best ideas are often a combination of several thoughts and ideas. To look at things on the ends of the spectrum can be a tragic mistake.

To overcome the either/or trust buster, I like to ask, "Can we find some compromise position here, even temporarily, that will allow us to take our discussion forward?"

2. Hard/Soft: Some leaders push for contributors to use facts, figures and analysis to prove their points. There is little or no room for intuition, insights or experience. This is a safe position for a leader to take and may make sense when dealing with younger and less experienced subordinates. But it certainly serves to shut down the willingness of someone to continue to offer ideas in the future.

To overcome the hard/soft trust buster, I like to say, "This is a new suggestion and I certainly can't prove it will work beyond a doubt. But the collective experience and intuition of the group makes us believe it is worth consideration. Can we discuss this further?"

3. Skepticism/Acceptance: Sometimes leaders think they add value by criticizing or nitpicking ideas or suggestions. It's a philosophy of "I'll tear them down to build them up later." What it means is they're unable to accept a different or counterintuitive idea or look for the worth in new perspectives. Sometimes you just need to "park your expectations" for a while. The reality is that if you cannot sort through recommendations and select the best elements without rejecting the whole idea, you will miss a lot and turn off a lot of people.

To overcome the skepticism/acceptance trust buster, I like to say, "I know you may be skeptical about this, but for purposes of this discussion, I am asking you to open yourself up to some different possibilities."

If you see any of these trust busters used to a significant extent in an organization or if you see all three to a modest extent, that organization will be characterized by pervasive mistrust. The effect of these trust busters is corrosive, and it wears down the willingness of others to contribute their ideas and suggestions. Anyone can encounter trust busters at any point in their life or career, but such environments are especially prevalent in the challenging work climate that we find ourselves in today. When everyone is overwhelmed with an avalanche of things to do, it is difficult to slow things down and consider ways to show that you are willing and able to listen as a leader. Since it can be riskier to try new things, these trust busters can also provide an effective, but ultimately counterproductive, method to "play it safe."

I have empathy for leaders in today's challenging work environment, but the disengagement currently felt by employees, especially millennials, may lead to substantial levels of turnover and disruption when the economy is more stable and the demand for workers increases. If you want to retain your best and brightest, it would be better to begin improving employee engagement now by overcoming the three trust busters.

Ask yourself:

- Can I say that I have been able to take advantage of good potential ideas from all parts of my team?

- Have I found ways to overcome trust busters and think that members of my team have demonstrated increased levels of commitment and engagement?

- Can I reinforce how my team has benefited from some different ideas or perspectives?

Passion versus Intensity:
The Impact on Leadership Effectiveness

We may affirm absolutely that nothing great in the world has ever been accomplished without passion.
—Georg Wilhelm Frederich Hegel

I have been working on trying to better understand the difference between leaders who are thought of as "intense" versus those who are considered "passionate." Lots of intense leaders think they are passionate, but they don't get the same personal satisfaction, sustained engagement, buy-in from their staff or level of connection with those they serve as do leaders who are truly passionate.

I have summarized the difference between the two styles in the following graphic:

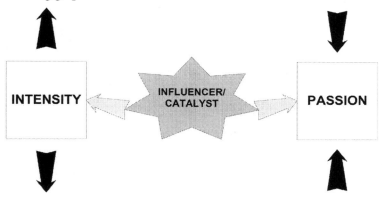

Leaders use their power to influence situations and the people and resources needed to accomplish things along the way. If you think of this like a chemical reaction, the leader is like a catalyst, something that can accelerate the rate of a reaction without getting consumed by it. Like actual chemicals, catalytic leaders can create intense reactions that throw off a lot of heat. We are naturally very cautious about getting too close to such intensity because we don't want to get "burned." Other leaders can approach similar situations and get things done without throwing off such heat. They create "warmth" that attracts others to engage or follow toward the leader's goal or objective. Both leaders get things done, but it is a very different experience for those being led.

A Passionate Leader—A Compelling Model

I have known Paul E. Purcell, Chairman of Robert W. Baird & Company, which is headquartered in Milwaukee, Wisconsin, for many years. Since being named president in 1998 and CEO in 2000, he has accomplished the following:

- Began an international expansion that now includes Europe and Asia;
- Saw revenue growth more than quadruple and exceed $1 billion per year;
- Took the company private in 2004, making it employee-owned, with a book value per share that has almost doubled since that time;
- Won accolades as one of *Fortune Magazine*'s "Top 100 Companies to Work For" over the last 14 years;
- Recognized by peers as the top middle-market investment bank and most trusted research group multiple times;
- Reinforced the value of putting clients first and demanding that teamwork is the way to succeed in the market with his "No Asshole Rule." (See page 33.)

I have seen Purcell grow as a leader and he has guided Baird with a firm, conservative hand that has taken a long-term view of what's in the best interests of the clients and employees.

Paul is an investment banker by training and has a nose for markets, trends and the art of the deal. He is passionate about his people, but he continually raises the bar on performance and holds people accountable for results. He empowers by developing and clarifying strategy with his senior leaders, zeroes in on supporting their tactical choices and is always available for consultation and dialogue. His team respects him deeply and does not want to disappoint him, but this is not hero worship. Paul is a hardnosed businessman who spends a lot of time on the human capital aspect of the business as well. He's intense about performance and passionate about people and the firm. He keeps Baird aligned to its purpose by carefully pruning the organization for profitable growth. He ensures the right attitude is consistently reflected, as is evidenced by his "No Asshole Rule." He is committed to soliciting input and connecting with employees and customers so that everyone can ensure they have the opportunity to add to the firm's success.

Passionate Suggestions for the Intense

Lao-tzu, a Chinese philosopher from the sixth century B.C., said, "A leader is best . . . when people barely know he exists. But of a good leader, who talks little, when his work is done, his aim fulfilled, they will say, 'We did this ourselves.'" When I think of the passion that good leaders can create, I think of three elements of the passionate style that create results and connections between leaders and their teams:

• **Alignment:** Because passionate leaders can attract others to their cause or purpose, they create alignment, a common purpose and focus:

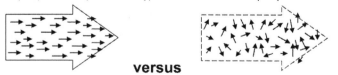

versus

• **Attitude:** Both passionate and intense leaders project a "can-do" attitude that is infectious and, therefore, mobilizes a team to perform. The key difference is that intense leaders can also create a subtle or not-so-subtle "or else" aspect to their messages. Followers of passionate leaders do not want to disappoint because they have bought into the project or effort and have allegiance to their leader. Followers of intense leaders may seek to conform or produce out of fear or self-preservation. Both approaches are effective from a results perspective, but they do not create the same sense of respect for or commitment to the leaders.

• **Additive:** Intense leaders can be so focused on a task and create time pressures for performing that executing the task is all you have time for. This robs the team of the chance to provide input and the opportunity to shape the outcome. Passionate leaders build in time for contribution and input and value what they hear, even if they do not choose to follow it all. People feel heard.

But even if intense leaders embrace alignment, attitude and being additive in their leadership style, key changes must be made to overcome the corrosive impact of the verbal, vocal and nonverbal elements of their communication. The condescension, belittling, intimidation and body language that support an intense leadership style must change over time. An intense leader who's intent on moving toward becoming more passionate should have a confederate who will provide feedback after meetings and discussions. We are not the best judges of the impact we have on others. We need the feedback!

The Values of Passion and Intensity

A critical question is whether passion or intensity is more effective in generating sustainable results and engagement in an organization. The answer depends on the situation you are dealing with and the time, criticality and risks associated with the potential outcomes. Although a passionate style creates the best long-term benefits, in times of crisis or urgency, some intensity is warranted.

The more intense style of leadership makes perfect sense when there are severe time constraints, significant cost overruns, impacts to organizational reputation due to client disruptions or when a team is responding to some business emergency due to uncontrollable events. The risks of shifting to a more intense model for a short time are limited if a pattern of a more participatory decision-making style has been established. When the crisis is over, you shift back to more passion and less intensity. You have established enough trust with your followers that you can be seen as flexible without being inconsistent.

Benjamin Disraeli, 19th century British Prime Minister, said, "Man is truly great when he acts from the passions." This is the central calamity of the passion versus intensity dichotomy: Intense leaders who are well intended and acting for the good of the organization and their team can be completely blindsided by how they are perceived. They feel as though they couldn't be more personally passionate about a task or challenge and would expect their team to have that perception of them. But the cumulative impact of their verbal, vocal and nonverbal behavior has left others with a different perspective. I often see this surprise in 360-degree feedback. Intense leaders may be just as passionate about their team and the work they do, and they are not in it to pad their resumes or get results no matter the impact on others. They hope people warm to them, but they may not experience that until they can shift their behavior.

The image of passionate leaders who wear their emotions on their sleeves and serve as cheerleaders for success rather than as effective business drivers is a misread of the style. Passionate leaders manage their passions and use them to everyone's advantage. Intense leaders let anger, frustration and impatience get the better of them and keep others at bay. The ability to sustain passion demands that the systems and processes are in place to make the results they are aiming for a reality. The intense leader may ask for his team to make process improvements and suggestions, but the team soon grows weary of trying because they usually fall short of the poorly expressed or unspoken expectations of the leader. There never seems to be time to work on the business together, so the cycle repeats itself with more anger, frustration and impatience on the part of the leader.

All the intensity with the attendant negativity, meanness and condescension to those who don't "get it" or disagree is just so much needless overkill that robs others of truly getting on board with a leader's true passion. The focus that accompanies a tough-minded discipline toward a goal helps everyone win; people can rally around that. The success Paul Purcell has created and sustained at Robert W. Baird is a testament to the return on investment of a truly passionate leader.

Ask yourself:

- Do I see myself as a passionate or an intense leader?

- Other than in times of crisis, does my team seem comfortable, yet respectful, in pushing back to ask me for clarification or to offer other ideas?

- Have I captured both minds and hearts as a leader?

I would like to thank John J. Pauly, PhD, Provost, Marquette University, Milwaukee, Wisconsin, for his support, encouragement and contributions to this chapter and Michael Adams, my friend and former client, for his editorial suggestions and moral support.

Keeping Calm in the Storm:
Wisdom from the "Zen Master"

In a controversy, the moment we feel anger, we have ceased striving for the truth and have begun striving for ourselves.

—Buddha

How often after you have been in a testy exchange with someone—a boss, a peer, a spouse or one of your children—do you ask yourself:

- How did I let that get away from me?
- Why did I lose my cool?
- Well, is that how I wanted that to turn out?
- I think I'm right, but that felt all wrong. Will it help this relationship?

Unfortunately, this situation happens to us all. I've seen some incredibly talented and successful executives lose their cool with people they really respect and seen the unfortunate fallout from it in damaged careers and relationships.

One leader I admire is Phil Jackson, whose book *11 Rings: The Soul of Success*,[38] is about his 11 NBA Championships with the Chicago Bulls and LA Lakers. He also won two while playing for the New York Knicks in the 1970s. He was referred to as the "Zen Master" by sportswriters because of his adherence to the practice of Zen Buddhism and how that influenced the selfless style of play he taught in a world of egomaniacal superstars. But his technique worked again and again on the court.

Jackson also wrote *Sacred Hoops: Spiritual Lessons of a Hardwood Warrior* in 1995. As a Bulls fan and admirer of Coach Jackson, I eagerly read it, and the following passage really hit a chord with me:

"In Zen it is said that the gap between accepting things the way they are and wishing them to be otherwise is 'the tenth of an inch of difference between heaven and hell.' If we can accept whatever we've been dealt—no matter how unwelcome—the way to proceed eventually becomes clear. This is what is meant by right action: the capacity to observe what's happening and act appropriately, without being distracted by self-centered thoughts. If we rage and resist, our angry, fearful minds have trouble quieting down sufficiently to allow us to act in the most beneficial way for ourselves and others."[39]

During a losing effort, one of Jackson's key players, Horace Grant, asked for extra help because the player he was guarding was having a career night and Grant knew he couldn't control him without some support. Jackson refused to listen to Grant or modify his defensive scheme. During the game, Grant became incensed with Jackson and even cursed him, behavior completely out of character for the devoutly religious Grant. The battle between player and coach caused them to lose the basketball game that night, a defeat that Jackson laid squarely on his own shoulders.

Jackson admitted that if he had stepped back and not let the issue become about his "stubborn resistance to playing defense a certain way," he would have seen that Grant was not questioning his authority or his coaching plans. He just had an unusual situation that called for some different thinking.

How often do you let your emotions get in the way of seeking the best solution? How often is it because the situation may call for a mid-course adjustment that throws your plans into disarray? How often does it set you off because it robs you of the control you thought you might have over a complex situation?

We all have emotional triggers—things that can really make us upset. Sometimes it's having our authority questioned. It can also be rudeness, lack of preparation or effort on others' parts or getting surprised by situations that you should have been aware of. Then it can be hard to have your "angry, fearful mind" calm down enough to take the emotion out of the equation. It doesn't mean you don't have a right to feel angry or fearful about how a situation is playing out. But as a leader, you must not let your emotions hijack the situation. That is what Jackson said happened to him in the situation with Horace Grant in that game.

Phil Jackson never says that keeping a cool head is easy, but he learned to do it in some of the most high-profile venues in the sporting world. His study of Zen Buddhism helped him in that regard, and his players responded to him remarkably well. *Sacred Hoops* is primarily about how Jackson was able to coach Michael Jordan to become the best teammate he could become, not just the best player.

When the seas are raging all around you and you know your triggers are being pushed . . .

Ask yourself:

- Why am I so upset right now?

- How do I find a way to step back and calm down?

- Who do I need to work with to reach a good solution as expeditiously as possible? This is a critical question, especially if the answer is the person you are angry at!

- If I could step outside and observe this situation from the view of a neutral third party, what would I see that is different from what I am seeing now?

Motivating Others—A Practical Approach

I do believe that in order to be a successful negotiator as a diplomat,
you have to be able to put yourself into the other person's shoes.
Unless you can understand what is motivating them, you are never going
to be able to figure out how to solve a particular problem.

—Madeleine Albright

A client who I had been working with for about a year was promoted from senior technical manager to director. His name, for purposes of this discussion, will be Bob. Bob is a technically gifted engineer with a remarkable work ethic and a great track record in his company (a key national cable organization). Bob is an empathic person with a good sense of humor. His team of a dozen engineers is responsible for systems that affect the whole national network. This is a role with lots to do and lots of pressure in an organization that sees all issues as high priority. It's a pressure-cooker environment.

Naturally, Bob, who is also a proud father of a couple of young children, is challenged to keep up with the demands of his job. When any leader I serve is challenged like this, one area we discuss is how you can delegate more effectively to help plan, prepare and keep up with demands while enduring less "pain and suffering." Bob and I discussed his challenges in detail, and I provided materials to assist him in thinking through things he could try to shift his behavior. Adjustment takes time, but with each modest success—for example, more time to prepare for a key meeting or letting a member of his team handle a task well that Bob would have done in the past—the path to improved delegation and its benefits for everyone became a beacon for not only growth but a sliver of sanity in a crazy world of work.

Regrettably, Bob did not stay on the path to mastering the art of delegation. Individuals must be motivated to change their behavior. There's a diagnostic tool called Expectancy Theory. (You can learn more about it at http://www.leadership-central.com/expectancy-theory-of-motivation.html#axzz3cZqRlp7n). Let's apply this tool to why Bob was resistant to delegating. First consider the following graphic regarding the likelihood that Bob will embrace delegation:

ABILITY	ABLE / NOT WILLING	ABLE / WILLING
	NOT ABLE / NOT WILLING	NOT ABLE / WILLING

WILLINGNESS

This is a way to examine how motivated someone might be to complete a task they have been given. If they are not able to perform a task, then this will either disqualify them from having that task delegated to them or identify that they are good candidates for training or mentoring. If they are able and willing, then let them perform the task. If they are able, but not willing, that becomes an issue of motivation. I assumed after detailed discussions that Bob would be both willing and able to learn to delegate more effectively. It seemed everyone would benefit from it, especially Bob. But my assumption turned out to be incorrect. This is where Expectancy Theory can be insightful.

Expectancy Theory was developed by Victor Vroom, a business school professor and sociologist, at the Yale School of Management, who was born in Montreal in 1932. He holds a Ph.D. from the University of Michigan. Vroom's primary research was on the Expectancy Theory of Motivation, which attempts to explain why individuals choose to follow certain courses of action in organizations, particularly in decision making and leadership. His most well-known books are *Work and Motivation, Leadership and Decision Making* and *The New Leadership*. Vroom has also been a consultant to corporations such as GE and American Express. This material was adapted from his theory.

Vroom created the Expectancy Theory in the 1960s. It maintains that work motivation is determined by individual beliefs regarding effort/performance, relationships and work outcomes. For instance, if you ask a member of your team to make a presentation to the executive team for you while you are out of town on business, you might expect he or she would jump at the chance for the exposure and the opportunity, since the topic is one about which he or she is knowledgeable. The employee, according to Vroom's theory, will determine his/her motivation to perform this task as follows:

$(E{\rightarrow}P)$: If I put forth the EFFORT, I can PERFORM the task of giving the presentation to the executive team. This judgment will have a lot to do with the person's comfort and ability as a presenter and knowledge of the subject.

$(P{\rightarrow}O)$: If I PERFORM the task, making the presentation, there will be an OUTCOME for it. This could be exposure or influence on a topic the employee feels strongly about.

V: The VALUE the EMPLOYEE places on the OUTCOME.

Therefore, the "equation" looks like this: $(E{\rightarrow}P) \times (P{\rightarrow}O) \times V =$ Motivation to perform the task. So from your perspective, this should be a plum assignment and opportunity for your employee. You believe he or she can do it based on having seen him/her in action elsewhere, and you believe anyone would want the exposure, so the value they would place on this opportunity should be high. They should be motivated to take the assignment.

What you don't know, and the employee may be afraid to admit, is that before you got here, your predecessor asked them do something much like this. They worked hard at the presentation but during its delivery, the meeting was interrupted with some challenging news. The attendees became less focused and started to throw out some unfair questions. As a result, the employee felt raked over the coals. It was not a pleasant experience! This is why you must analyze Expectancy Theory from the employee's perspective and not project your values or confidence onto them. Just because you value something does not mean they will. This tool and these questions can then be useful to assist you in preparing and moving a member of the team to higher levels of motivation.

With this model in mind, what created Bob's reluctance to delegate? Let's break it down:

(E→P): If Bob puts forth the effort he can perform the task:

- It would take Bob longer to explain than just do the task himself.
- Clarity on many tasks was a work in progress. Bob felt he could keep most of these things working in his head and adjust on the fly rather than taking the time to update his team members as things progressed.
- Bob is a very empathic person. Although he was being bombarded, he did not want to burden his team any more that he had to.

(P→O): If Bob performs the task of delegating, there will be outcomes for it:

- Bob could gain more time to plan, prepare and sell his ideas.
- He already felt out of the loop on some issues and this

would make it worse. Bob had not figured out how to have whomever he delegated to keep him up to speed.

- Bob was worried that he would lose his technical currency by being less directly involved in all technical discussions.

V: The value Bob places on the outcome.

- On a net basis, it's pretty low. That's why Bob resisted.

The most critical thing to understand about the Expectancy Theory is that you cannot project what you may value as being motivating for someone else. You have to dig down and understand where the other person is coming from. Bob's boss and I have helped him overcome some of his resistance and he's on his way to being a more effective delegator and leader.

How to Use This Tool

As you prepare for an interaction with an employee or colleague, break down the request you have for them and use the following questions to make better use of Expectancy Theory in reaching an agreement that will work for both sides.

Performance

- Do I know what I want the employee to do?
- Is it important that the employee do it? If not, is it worth the effort?
- Can I communicate it so the employee understands it?
- If the employee does it, how will I be able to observe or confirm that it's been accomplished?

(E→P) Beliefs (If I try, I can do it.)

- What can I do to reinforce or increase the employee's self-confidence?
- Can I get others (possibly my boss) to express confidence in the employee?

- What past successes of the employee can I cite? How does this task differ from past successes or failures? How can I help improve the employee's ability?
- What support can I provide to the employee?
- How can I restructure the task to make it easier or more manageable, or at least to appear so to the employee? Can I break the performance change objective into sub-tasks? How can I provide positive feedback for the accomplishment of these sub-tasks?
- Am I a positive model for my employee?

(P→O) Beliefs (If I do it, I'll get something for it.)
- What outcomes do I want to add?
- Have I considered intrinsic as well as extrinsic outcomes?
- Are all the outcomes realistic?
- How much power do I have to make sure the outcomes happen? What can I do to make sure they happen? If I don't have power over certain outcomes, what assurances can I get from those who do?
- Which positive outcomes do I want to emphasize or make more attractive?
- Which negative outcomes do I want to de-emphasize or eliminate?
- How can I convince the employee that the outcomes will happen? What past experiences of the employee can I cite?

V Beliefs (What I get is attractive or of value to me.)
- How can I influence the value the employee places on outcomes?
- How can I show that outcomes the employee perceives as negative are really not so bad or possibly of positive value?
- How can I link outcomes that have low value to the employee with those that have greater value?

- What problem solving can I do with the employee to help reduce the probability that negative outcomes will follow?

Ask yourself:

- Do I understand how motivated a member of my team may to be achieve a task?
- Do they believe they can accomplish it well?
- What outcomes/rewards do they expect to receive from stepping up to this task?
- Do I understand the value they place on stepping up to this task?

TRANSACTIONAL ANALYSIS:
A MODEL FOR EFFECTIVE COMMUNICATIONS

In the last analysis, what we are communicates far more
eloquently than anything we say or do.
—STEPHEN COVEY

TRANSACTIONAL ANALYSIS WAS created by psychotherapist Eric Berne, M.D., (1910–1970) from studies he conducted in the 1950s. It made complex interpersonal transactions understandable when he recognized that people can interact from one of three "ego-states": parent, adult and child.

Each of the ego states is a system of communication with its own language and function; the parent's is a language of values; the adult's is a language of logic and rationality; and the child's is a language of emotions.

Berne's most famous book, *Games People Play*,[40] opened a new area of understanding about the complexity of overt and covert interpersonal communication. To enhance their appreciation of the intended or unintended impact of their communication efforts, leaders can learn a few key things from Berne's theories.

First, consider these three elements of transactional communication:

• We possess all three ego states in our consciousness. Your personality is a result of your cumulative life experiences. Who you are as a parent, adult or child is a function of these experiences, no matter how you may wish to depart from them. You and whoever you are communicating with are who you are.

261

- Although we can learn new behaviors and skills, often what we intend in a transaction is not how the receiver interprets it.
- All ego states are okay in business dealings, but you need to be sure you are using each as you intend!

Ego States and Transactions

People's interactions are made up of transactions. Transactions have two parts: the stimulus and the response. Individual transactions are usually part of a larger set. Transactional sets or sequences can be direct, productive and healthy or they can be devious, wasteful and unhealthy.

People interact in one of three ego states. An ego state is a specific way of thinking, feeling and behaving, and each ego state has its origin in specific regions of the brain. People can behave from their parent, adult or child ego state.

1. **The Parent:** The parent is like a tape recorder. It is a collection of prerecorded, predetermined, codes for living. When you are in the parent ego state, you think, feel and behave like your parents or someone who took their place. The parent decides, without reasoning, how to react to situations, what is good or bad and how people should live. When the parent transaction is critical, Berne calls it the critical parent. When it is supportive it is called the nurturing parent.

2. **The Adult:** When in the adult ego state, you function as a human computer. You operate on data you collect and store or use to make decisions according to a logic-based program. When in the adult ego state, you use logical thinking to solve problems, making sure that child or parent emotions do not contaminate the process.

3. **The Child:** When you are in the child ego state, you act like the child you once were. You aren't just putting on an act; you

think, feel, see, hear and react as a child. The child transaction tends to be self-centered, emotional and resistant to the suppression filters that come with growing up.

Complementary and Cross Transactions

Transactions occur when any person relates to any other person. Each transaction is made up of a stimulus and a response, and transactions can proceed from the parent, adult or child of one person to the parent, adult or child of another person. In Berne's model, the sender is the one who initiates the transaction or the communication interaction. There is always a receiver of the communication and the overall reaction is either complementary or crossed.

A complementary transaction involves the same ego state in each person. In a crossed transaction, the transactional response is addressed to an ego state different from the sender's. Communication can continue between two adults as long as transactions are complementary; crossed transactions are important to analyze because they disrupt communication.

Complementary Transactions

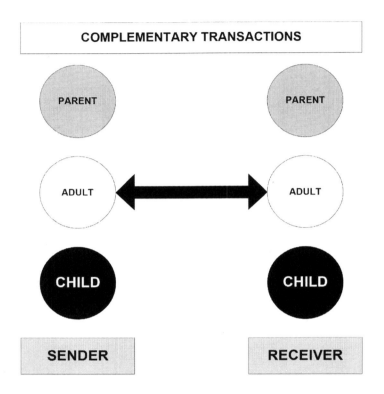

Since the adult ego state is all about logic and rationality, we would ideally like to ensure that all communications in the work-place are adult–adult. After all, we are all supposed to act like adults and that should be the basis for our communications in the workplace. In reality, it often doesn't work that way, so let's examine crossed transactions.

Crossed Transactions

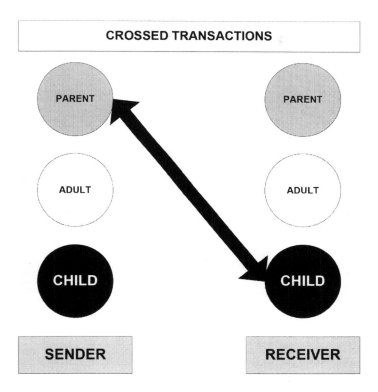

In a crossed transaction, the most frequently problematic issue is the parent–child communication.

In the crossed example above, where you (the sender) are speaking to one of your staff (the receiver), it is coming across as a parent–child transaction. There can be many reasons for this type of communication, but think of it diagnostically from each perspective:

Sender as Parent
- You have had to follow up several times about a deliverable, so you are frustrated with your staff member's performance. You are impatient, and your disappointment is clear in your voice and body language.
- You are anxious about getting a big assignment done and need the input of your staff. They may or may not be aware of the pressure you are under, but your tension comes across.
- You are very good at details and often have valuable insights, so you review things in detail and almost always have suggestions for everything your team does.

Receiver as Child
- I'm trying here and I feel I have disappointed the parent figure.
- My boss sounds like my parents when I was a teenager and came home after curfew.
- I feel that my boss may not trust me to perform adequately, even though I have been doing the work for some time.

The key is to heighten your awareness of how your communication is being received. If you get into the parent–child mode too often with a subordinate, it can be frustrating for both you and the employee, since you'll lose confidence and the employee will feel belittled. Consider the relationships you have established with your team members.

Ask yourself:

- Do my communications fit the team and are people responsive to my style?

- Have I invested enough time for them to understand my expectations?

- Do my team members have the skills and training they need to succeed? Can they do what I am asking?

FOCUS ON IMPACT, NOT ACTIVITY:
A MODEL FOR IMPROVING
CUSTOMER SATISFACTION

*Develop success from failures. Discouragement and failure
are two of the surest stepping stones to success.*
—DALE CARNEGIE

I GOT A NOTE FROM a friend with whom I had done some work on
Habitat for Humanity projects over the years. She and her team
were looking for ways to get a fresh look at how to present their
value proposition to a long-standing client who had decided to put
the work out for bid. The situation was not a negative reflection on
my friend's organization; the client was just "kicking tires" to see
what was out there.

We chatted about the need to ensure that clients consistently
believe they are getting value for their dollar. I mentioned to my
friend that a useful way of representing their contributions for this
longer-term, retainer relationship was to focus on not just what
they did for the client—the activities—but to carefully link activities to the outcomes, or the impact, of the work they did. Often
your contributions can be taken for granted and it's worth the time
for both parties to clarify and reinforce how the client benefits from
the relationship.

I work with a fellow named Zack who handles my search engine
optimization and social media work. I admire Zack and enjoy working with him but actually have very little idea what the activities are
that he engages in. But the impacts are clearly delineated in the various metrics that can be discerned from his work. I suggested that
it would be advantageous to my friend to restate what the intended

benefits, or impacts, are for her client and to solicit feedback about the level of satisfaction with each. So the process flows like this:

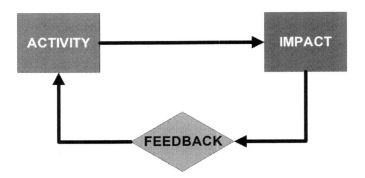

The benefits for my friend's firm as they analyze the activities they engage in are as follows:

- Clarifying the various activities that result in each impact for the client;
- Providing the opportunity to think about the efficiency of each internal process in creating the various impacts;
- Matching the efficiency of their internal processes to the perceived benefits of each impact from the client's perspective;
- If the impacts do not seem to be valued by the client, or do not seem to measure up to the standards the client demands, that may mean:

  ○ My friend's company needs to improve the caliber of their activities;
  ○ They need to stop activities that the client doesn't value;
  ○ They need to revisit the goals or intent of the client for each element of this work;
  ○ Or some combination of the above.

I realize that engaging in this kind of exercise while you are in the midst of completing an RFP to retain an important account is not easy. But it is an important exercise that vendors like my friend and I must engage in regularly with our clients.

Several years ago I was engaged in a retainer relationship with an important client. I had coached a fairly large number of people within that organization over several years. Many were at senior levels. I made it a point to stay in touch with my former clients even after the regular coaching assignment was concluded because I was convinced they valued these interactions. I approached the CEO as well as the head of Human Capital and they agreed to a modest monthly retainer to compensate me for my efforts. This arrangement went fine for a couple of years.

A new head of Talent Development, who managed the use of coaches for the firm, and the head of Human Capital asked me to join them for lunch. I came prepared with a full accounting of all my activities for all the clients I met with. It clearly showed that my total time spent with the clients exceeded the retainer payments. And I assumed that the impact of my work was viewed positively. But I did not ask them about that. After the meeting, I felt I had missed something but let it go. Within a year, the retainer program ended. That does not mean I did not continue to get work from the client, but in retrospect, I see now that I missed an opportunity to learn more about the client's mindset and how I could have been an even more valuable resource.

As you reflect on the satisfaction of your clients, ask yourself:

- What have the notable impacts been for the various activities I provide to my clients, internal or external?

- How do I measure how my clients value these activities?

- How often do I use the client's feedback to assist in improving my processes or product?

- Am I afraid to hear what the client is really thinking?

.

EMPATHY IN BUSINESS:
OVERCOMING THE DISTANCE BETWEEN YOURSELF AND OTHERS

Empathy is about finding echoes of another person in yourself.
—MOSHIN HAMID

I spoke with a client about the difference between having power and having influence. He does not command a large staff or budget, but he leads a technical team that manages a specialized type of interface that was critical to many products. So he doesn't make things happen by his power but by his ability to influence other people. To expand and re-inforce his influence, he and I spoke about making the time to connect with users of his team's products to understand them better.

This issue of influence and others was at the heart of a remarkable film, "Selma," which I saw on the holiday commemorating Dr. Martin Luther King, Jr. It is a fantastic film that not only brings to life the struggles and accomplishments of the great civil rights leader but also brings into focus how "other" the blacks and whites were to each other in the American South in 1965.

Another example of this "otherness" was portrayed in the recent book by Laura Hillenbrand, *Unbroken*, about an American prisoner of war in a Japanese camp as World War II came to an end. The last example comes from a book by Eric Larson, *In The Garden of Beasts*, based on the true story of a mild-mannered University of Chicago history professor who became the U.S. Ambassador to Germany in 1933, just as Hitler rose to power.

These true stories reflected the sincere belief that the "others" were inferior to the group doing the judging. In each case, these cultural assumptions had racial foundations. In the American South, whites

271

were convinced of their superiority to blacks, and those cultural assumptions were reflected in how life was organized. Both the Japanese and German peoples were convinced that they were a master race, and their cultural assumptions were inculcated from an early age. In each case, other people were lesser in their eyes.

In *In the Garden of Beasts*, Ambassador William Dodd and his family were struck by the contrast between the strict German laws against animal cruelty and the treatment of Jewish and Gypsy citizens. They were impressed with how German pets were so well treated and appalled at the cruelty of regular German citizens to the "others" in their midst.

The differences between people in the workplace are never as stark, passionate or destructive as the racial divides that are reflected in the three previous examples. But lack of understanding of other teams or groups does lead to its own set of challenges and problems. So how do you overcome the distance between yourself and others you work with? I can sum it up in one word: empathy. Empathy is often referred to as putting yourself in someone else's shoes, to see if you can connect to what they may be feeling. In business interactions, empathy is often less about sharing others' feelings and more about understanding others' vision, goals and objectives. That understanding can help you better focus on commonalities and create a better foundation for resolving differences.

I recently had a client who approached a leader in another part of the organization. There's a great amount of interdependence between the functions of my client and this other manager. My client went to the other leader's office, sat down and spent about 30 minutes just asking questions and seeking to be sure that he understood the challenges and needs of that manager and his team. At the end of 30 minutes, he thanked the other individual for his time and prepared to depart. The other manager got up and stood between the door and my client and pointedly asked, "So why did you really come here? What's going on and what do you need from me?" "Nothing but the information you gave me, which helps me better understand how I can work better with you and your team," said my client. The other manager actually seemed baffled by this approach. It takes effort to break down barriers, especially mistrust.

I came across an interesting article, "Six Habits of Highly Empathic People,"[41] by Roman Krznaric, formerly a professor of sociology and politics at Cambridge University. Here are the four most pertinent habits he listed for you to consider to make yourself a more empathic leader in the workplace:

1. **Cultivate curiosity about strangers:** Develop an insatiable curiosity about others, but don't interrogate them. Ask them about where they're from, what they do and what might lead them to believe what they're saying. Krznaric quotes Studs Terkel, the oral historian, "Don't be an examiner; be an interested inquirer."

2. **Challenge prejudices and discover commonalities:** Krznaric says, "Highly empathic people challenge their own preconceptions and prejudices by searching for what they share with people rather than what divides them." Don't automatically gravitate toward what separates you, but try to reinforce similar beliefs, experiences and perspectives. Recognizing what's similar or common makes differences seem less extreme.

3. **Listen hard and open up:** Practice active listening and ensure that you have thoroughly grasped at least the essence of another's perspective or understanding before you respond. Use clarifying questions to dig deeper and simply pause before you respond. If someone else senses that you are developing your response rather than deeply listening, they will eventually turn off.

4. **Try another person's life:** Walking in another's shoes may be difficult, but it can take many forms. I serve with a group of people who provide dinner at a homeless shelter each month,

making the meal, serving it and sitting with the men to learn more about their state in life. It's opened my eyes to the plight of the homeless in many ways. A cable company I know of gives senior technical employees the opportunity to ride with an installer to get a sense of the connection with the company's clients. Such short-term experiences can't tell you everything, but they can broaden your understanding and empathy.

Ask yourself:

• Who do I need to know better? How can I use empathy to connect more effectively?

• Do I have any prejudices about other teams, functions or individuals that get in the way of having the open mind I need to connect better?

• Who are five people I could connect with that would allow me to practice being empathic and potentially create mutually significant benefits? Will I take the next step and reach out?

Your Opinion—Is It Worth It?

No, I will be the pattern of all patience; I will say nothing.
—William Shakespeare

It's important to know that you can enhance your relationships by actually saying less at certain times rather than saying more. Jeff Immelt, CEO of General Electric, mentioned in a 2003 *Fast Company*[42] article that he purposely will "leave a few things unsaid in various meetings. I may know an answer, but I'll often let the team find its own way. Sometimes, being an active listener is much more effective than ending a meeting with me enumerating 17 actions." Immelt's philosophy can be very valuable and it's unfortunate that this attitude is not more common among leaders.

Marshall Goldsmith is perhaps the preeminent executive leadership coach in the United States. He has written a dozen or more books and served as an executive coach to leaders of many key international organizations. His *New York Times* best-selling book *What Got You Here Won't Get You There*[43] identifies 20 habits that hold you back from the top. The first one is "winning too much." One common attribute of successful executives is their highly competitive natures. It is not accidental that people who are driven to win and succeed are the ones who move up and lead organizations. The problem is that sometimes strengths carried to the extreme can become vices. In other words, we can't seem to turn off or moderate our competitive juices when winning may not matter that much or when pushing to get our way becomes counterproductive.

Senior leaders tend to be pretty sharp cookies. Certain skill deficiencies or character flaws may present themselves after many years, but you don't get to the upper rungs of organizations if you don't have the intellectual horsepower to play at that level. So sometimes in the give-and-take of meetings or in discussions, some people just can't help showing off, topping what might have been another excellent idea put forth by others. This tendency is a combination of what Goldsmith calls habit number two, *"adding too much value,"* and number six, *"telling the world how smart we are."*

These are closely related. I think some people, especially those of us reared in the American culture, feel compelled to act this way because competition rather than collaboration has been drilled into us from a very young age. We are also a society that is more individualistic than collectivist in our orientation to the world.

Competition Rather Than Collaboration

When my son was in instructional soccer as a kindergartner, there were no goalies and no score was kept; it was all about developing skills and interest in the game. But rarely did we leave a match where I didn't hear a dad say something like, "Boy, you guys really put it to them today!" (Remember, this is completely against the intent and purpose of 6-year-olds just learning the game.) We also compete for the best grades, in activities and even for attention from parents, all starting at a very young age. This competitive zeal is fostered early, especially in the American culture.

How Perfectionists Are Challenged

As much as I hate to admit it, I am a bit of a perfectionist, although my zest for control of things in life has diminished greatly over the years. In my work with my clients, a couple of assessments that I use can point out if an individual has tendencies toward perfectionism in their personality. This trait often can be a good thing because perfectionists get things done and pay great attention to quality and detail; however, too great a need for control can stifle people and organizations and leave people consistently unsatisfied with the quality of their work.

I have used an excellent book called *Too Perfect: When Being in Control Gets Out of Control* by Allan Mallinger and Jeanette DeWyze[44] to understand this topic better and have recommended it to many of my clients whose personalities demonstrate a need for control that becomes counterproductive. The book has a 25-question quiz that can let you know how much of a perfectionist you might be. When my daughters were about 19 and 17, we sat in our kitchen and I read each of the questions to them and had them tally up their answers. I learned two sobering things that afternoon: Both my daughters had developed reasonably high levels of control orientation, and they were competing with each other for who could answer yes to the most questions.

I mention this personal anecdote because it reinforces this issue of competition versus collaboration. My experience with introducing total quality management to the Consumer Electronics Division of the RCA Corporation earlier in my career taught me a lot about the tools and techniques that go into group problem-solving and the effective collaboration it enables. Tools like brainstorming, the nominal group technique for sorting through a large number of options, and other approaches allow collaboration to flourish. If you are not naturally collaborative, use the tools you can find to assist you in making collaborative decisions.

How to Assess "Is It Worth It?"

As a senior leader, you must set an example of restraint by not allowing yourself to overwhelm the suggestions and ideas of others, especially your subordinates. In a February 17, 2014, blog titled "Is It Worth It?"[45] Goldsmith suggests that leaders listen to the suggestions and recommendations of others in meetings and consistently ask themselves whether it is really worth adding their ideas or perspectives. If adding your own ideas will diminish the suggestions of others or send a signal that you're more interested in what you have to say than in what others bring to the table, you should keep quiet.

Naturally, you should speak up if you have a genuinely better idea or if another suggestion has a flaw in reasoning or content that you have unique knowledge about. You owe it to everyone to contribute your ideas then.

Ask yourself:

- Is the suggestion on the table effective and adequate?

- Is my suggestion or idea so unique or compelling that the risks of overwhelming the ideas of my peers or my team are worth it?

- Am I throwing my idea out there simply because my competitive juices are flowing or because I have some unique knowledge or perspective to add?

- Is it in my best interest to show my collaborative and cooperative nature by not trumping another person's idea but rather showing support for the contributions of others?

WHAT'S WRONG WITH BEING PASSIVE-AGGRESSIVE?

Don't make assumptions. Find the courage to ask questions and
to express what you really want. Communicate with others as clearly as
you can to avoid misunderstandings, sadness and drama. With just this
one agreement, you can completely transform your life.
—MIGUEL ANGEL RUIZ

A CLIENT ASKED ME, "What's wrong with being passive-aggressive?" when we were discussing how he needed to be more consistently assertive in his workplace interactions. There was obvious confusion about what the term passive-aggressive means. I believe you can never be too assertive, but you have to understand the distinction between assertiveness and being aggressive or passive-aggressive.

My client was actually considering the concept of passive-aggressiveness in light of his reflection on a particularly contentious discussion within his team about paths to pursue regarding some pivotal challenges. He regretted being less aggressive about his thoughts and perspectives during the dialogue about these challenges. He also recognized the need to be passive when the boss got on his soapbox about what he wanted to do. There is a lot of confusion about the differences among these three positions and I use the chart on the next page to demonstrate them.

The "I'm OK, You're OK" model came from a book with the same title by Thomas A. Harris, M.D., that was published in 1969 and sold more than 15 million copies.[46]

• **Assertive:** The "I'm OK, you're OK" stance indicates that you believe that you have wants, needs, and desires and that you're going to

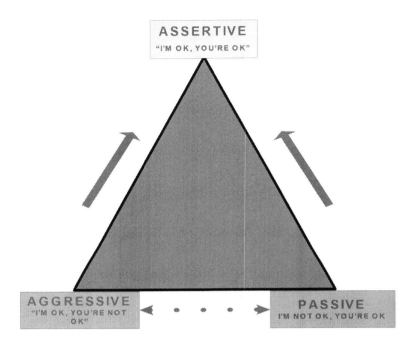

do everything in your power to fulfill them. But you recognize that others have their own needs and desires and have the right to equally pursue them. You understand that getting along usually requires dialogue and often compromise. You also understand some things are nonnegotiable, needs that you or the other person will not give up. But because you value the perspectives and needs of others, it sets an effective tone for balanced negotiation and dialogue.

• **Aggressive:** Aggressiveness means you're going to pursue your needs and desires regardless of any impact on others or their needs. Aggressiveness has its place on battlefields and athletic fields, and it currently seems to be the primary model in politics. But the "I'm OK, you're not OK" model does not build healthy and effective long-term relationships because one side consistently seeks to press its will on others.

• **Passive:** It may sound odd for many people to hear anyone say, "I'm not OK and you are." There are a host of reasons that someone may choose this path and many of them are psychological in nature. Working with a passive manager is often one of the most frustrating positions for an individual. Passive teammates are usually less of an issue because even assertive folks will push past them if they consistently fail to assert their rights. The disappointment here is that you do not get supportive action or useful perspective from passive people.

In her book, *Mastering Assertiveness Skills*,[47] Elaina Zuker suggested the following to help us understand the basics of being assertive:

ASSERTIVE BILL OF RIGHTS
- I have the right to be treated with respect.
- I have the right to have and express my own feelings and opinions.
- I have the right to be listened to and taken seriously.
- I have the right to set my own priorities.
- I have the right to say no without feeling guilty.
- I have the right to ask for what I want.
- I have the right to get what I pay for.
- I have the right to make mistakes.
- I have the right to assert myself even though I may inconvenience others.
- I have the right to choose not to assert myself.

These rights may seem self-evident—to borrow from a famous document—but they require confidence and conviction to live by.

Passive-Aggressive

Referring to the diagram, you'll see that lines lead from both being aggressive and being passive toward being assertive, meaning both those types should strive to achieve more assertive qualities. A dotted arrow connects aggressiveness with passiveness. If someone is counseled about being too aggressive, he or she may retreat to doing very little and being passive. However, this is not their natural state and the aggressiveness will leak out. If someone is encouraged to be more assertive, when he has traditionally been passive, he may overdo it and seem aggressive. And thus people will flip-flop between the passive and aggressive modes of behavior. Passive-aggressive behavior is often demonstrated in snide or denigrating comments, subtle accusations and mean-spirited or cutting humor. Input seems fairly indirect, but it is usually profoundly negative.

Because aggressive and passive types both create conflicts and tensions for assertive types, choosing the assertive path is rarely easy. If everyone were assertive and sought to collaborate, things would be easier. Being assertive may not always be popular, but it will be respected.

Ask yourself:

- What's my primary mode of behavior among these three styles?

- What have I done either too aggressively or passively and why did I choose each path at that time?

- When have I effectively asserted myself and how can I seek to make that my normal mode of behavior?

- What's one thing I can do today to enhance my assertiveness?

Three Steps to Giving as a Leader

The delicate balance of mentoring someone is not creating them in your own image but giving them the opportunity to create themselves.
—Steven Spielberg

Thanksgiving begins the holiday season and focuses on giving thanks for the bounty we have in our lives. Much of the rest of the holiday season focuses on giving. We give parties, we give bonuses (hopefully) and we plan our gift-giving for our loved ones. Okay, I must admit we all think a little bit about the getting as well!

In *Give and Take: A Revolutionary Approach to Success,*[48] Adam Grant, a professor at the University of Pennsylvania, sees people as givers, takers and matchers. Takers are often Machiavellians who are interested in only what's in it for them. Givers provide their personal and professional gifts to others freely without being overly concerned about what's in it for them. Matchers are in the middle and often weigh the cost-benefit of giving to others.

Grant refers to a study in which individuals were given $20 and told they must spend it by no later than 5 p.m. that day. They could spend it on themselves or others. The question was, "Who would be happier?" Individuals who spent the money on themselves found no discernible increase in their own happiness. But those who gave the money to others stated that they were significantly happier.

The positive effects of giving to others are reflected in a variety of literature. Grant refers to this as "otherish" giving, when you choose where, who and how you would like to help others, and it generally improves your mood. Economists refer to the "warm glow of giving" and psychologists refer to the "helper's high." Neuroscience provides evidence that giving affects the reward centers in our brains, sending us pleasure and purpose signals. Giving your time to help others also has a profound impact. Grant also notes that a "study of 2800 Americans over age 24 showed that volunteering predicted increases in happiness, life satisfaction and self-esteem—and decreases in depression—a year later."

But think of what we as leaders can give to the folks who work for us. Now if you could hand out large pay increases, bonuses or more impressive titles, I'm sure that would be well received by your staff. But in flatter organizations and in times of fiscal uncertainty, that is often not so easy to do.

So as a leader, what can you give to members of your team, especially your budding superstars, without breaking the bank? Here are three steps to giving you can consider:

1. Be a good manager and leader: Be a good role model as an effective listener, delegator, planner, communicator and meeting leader. Demonstrate support for ongoing development and appreciation of accomplishments. Working for a great boss can be critical in career development. Working for a bad boss is also enlightening about what not to do. You choose!

2. Think about what you can do to provide training, career advice, exposure and visibility. Team members benefit from attending certain meetings or working on assignments that stretch their perspectives and abilities. Can you be a mentor to some of your team and expose them to others within or outside of the organization, leading to new ideas and opportunities that they can apply in their current roles?

3. Consider being an "accountability coach" to those you provide this support to. Be willing to:

   • Debrief with them after networking you helped organize or a meeting you asked them to attend with or without you. Your time is a great gift; use it to help them think through what they experienced.

- Ask them what they learned and how they think they might use it to grow in their current roles. Have them identify one thing they will try to do differently based on what they were exposed to.
- Set up a schedule to review progress. These do not have to be extensive discussions, but show your continued interest. Have them set up the meetings and lead them. Just listen!

Ask yourself:

- Do I know what each member of my team really needs from me?

- What can I do that will cost me and my company virtually nothing but my time? What's that worth to me and my team?

- Can I learn to be a good "accountability coach"?

A Four-Stage Model for Managing Your Performance and Career

Life is about not knowing, having to change, taking the moment and making the best of it, without knowing what's going to happen next.

—Gilda Radner

In my work as an executive leadership coach, I have had many conversations with clients about the arc of their careers and the logical next steps for them to consider. Although career coaching has not been a focus of my work, I believe I have an important framework for you to use in analyzing where you stand in your career at any given moment.

In 1965, a psychologist named Bruce Tuckman developed a description of the path that high-performing teams follow in coming together and getting things done. He referred to this as "forming, storming, norming, and performing."[49] Although Tuckman was primarily interested in temporary working groups, I believe that this framework is helpful in understanding the development of permanent as well as newly formed teams. Here's a brief definition of each of these stages:

Forming: This is when workgroups or teams come together for particular projects, goals or purposes. Many people may be excited about working on the task ahead and others may have some trepidations or concerns. As a leader, your job is to understand and communicate the goals or purposes and ensure that there is as much alignment in that direction as possible on everyone's part.

Storming: In this phase, how the group will work together starts to gel. Issues of governance, problem solving, communication and goal setting are all on the table. People with different types of experiences and ideas come together and, as can be expected, the many differences of opinion can result in frictions large and small. The steady hand of the leader is essential to guide everyone forward in setting the ground rules for how they will operate.

Norming: This is the stage at which hierarchy becomes established, respect for the authority of the leader begins to solidify and roles and responsibilities are clarified. Although it depends on the task or focus of the work, wise leaders seek as much shared leadership as possible, especially so the various key skills, abilities and experiences of all members of the group can be brought into play. There is often a prolonged level of overlap between storming and norming behavior, especially as new tasks or challenges emerge. Hopefully, as the team learns to trust one another, this process becomes more natural and efficient.

Performing: In performing, all the hard work of the previous three phases comes together in fulfilling the shared vision of executing the goal. The structures and processes that have been established are facilitated by the individuals in their roles with the right responsibilities to get the job done. This becomes, in essence, the status quo.

Although Tuckman created the forming, storming, norming, and performing model (FSNP) for the development of high-performing teams, I believe it is just as relevant in looking at any organizational structure and providing fresh eyes for new goals, processes or structures that need to be established and implemented. Our work world reflects the volatility of current world situations and the inherent "creative destruction" that makes change our constant companion. If leaders are not consistently reflecting on how to incorporate new technology, people, systems and processes, they will ultimately hit a wall that they are unprepared for. Although no one should have any real confidence in the ability to predict how changes will influence what happens, it is important that you are always on the lookout and anticipating.

Here are some additional applications of the FSNP model for you to consider as you anticipate next steps on a project, diagnose an organizational challenge or plan for a needed change:

Forming: Welcome. Integrate. Focus.
- Introduction of new team members.
- Create focus and goals for new projects or initiatives.
- Embrace different ideas for how you are organized and use all the assembled talents.

Storming: Brainstorm. Debate. Create a Sense of Community/ Connection.
- Bring the light of day to any unease or friction the new situation creates.
- Discuss how you will treat each other, communicate and reach decisions.
- Keep the vision/goal in focus.
- Decide how you will measure success and how you keep everyone informed about it.

Norming: Clarify. Communicate. Do Not Assume Everyone "Gets It."
- Communicate what has been decided about what.
- Capture what has been decided about people, process and performance: Publish and proclaim it. You can't communicate too much.
- Make time for "post mortems" so you can constantly improve processes.

Performing: Execute. Reflect. Measure. Repeat.
- Celebrate success, and confront failure constructively.
- Reinforce how your team's efforts align with the strategic direction of the group or firm. Educate everyone.
- Fine tune metrics, goals and tactics constantly. Seek continuous improvement.

- Always "bring the outside in" to stay informed about the competition and best practices.

From a career perspective, I think the FSNP model is relevant throughout your career but especially once you have become established, midcareer and beyond. I think it's always important to evaluate the impact of change on you personally, your team and the organization.

If you join a new organization or venture, get a new job or assume new responsibilities in your current organization or are asked to participate in a new initiative, project or task force, each of the four phases of the development of the team come into play. It is a cycle that constantly repeats itself. I strongly encourage you to be appropriately selfish in your focus on the impact of all this on you first. Secondly, what are the positive and negative impacts for your team? Lastly, ask the same question about the effects on the organization. There should be substantial pluses or advantages for you individually that serve as a motivator for you. Ultimately there should be good alignment of the positive impacts for your team and the organization. I believe FSNP is an excellent diagnostic model for you to consider the impact of any change personally or organizationally.

It's always valuable to know where you stand in terms of the four stages of development for yourself and your team. Given the broad nature of a leader's responsibilities, some elements of the work will be performing very well. But there always will be areas that call for ongoing improvement or where you anticipate substantial changes may be in the offing. Be prepared to use this diagnostic tool to break these challenges down and gain some insight about how to transform, improve, or evolve the work and the people who conduct it.

Ask yourself:

- What stage of FSNP am I in currently in any projects or transitions I'm involved with?

- Am I resilient in dealing with the inherent ambiguity created by moving through the various stages of FSNP? What can I do to better prepare myself?

- Have I met someone who seems to "roll with the punches" well as teams are forming? Would I be willing to ask them to share how they do what they do?

HOW TO JUMP START YOUR NETWORKING

There is no such thing as a "self-made" man. We are made up of thousands of others. Everyone who has ever done a kind deed for us, or spoken one word of encouragement to us, has entered into the make-up of our character and of our thoughts, as well as our success.

—GEORGE BURTON ADAMS

ONE OF THE KEY AREAS of focus of my executive leadership coaching work centers on building, maintaining and enhancing relationships. Leaders exert influence through the relationships they have established, internally and externally to their organizations and within their field or industry. The most influential leaders, whether they occupy key positions in various organizations, or are regarded as "thought leaders" in their field, "work" their network in a disciplined manner on a regular basis. When you consider how busy you are with everything you have in your work life, not to mention your personal life (remember that?), you may wonder how they do it. Over time, you can come up with many reasons you do not have a network or work the one you have. Here are some excuses you may have heard or use yourself:

- I have no time for that!
- It's not as important as my work for my company.
- It's disloyal to my company, since the real purpose is to look for another job!
- I'm pretty good at what I do and have no time to do this, so how would someone else have the time to talk with me, much less have lunch?

- I've never really done this before. What would I talk about? Why would someone else want to speak with me?

I am sure you have heard others too, but these are excuses and do not reflect the reality of the way the world works today. The pace and severity of change in our world has created a need for a different and expanded way of looking at our work and how we accomplish things. The explosion of information and "flattening" of the economic landscape requires you to have a network of contacts to understand and develop shared meaning so you can keep up on what's happening in your field or industry and keep tabs on current and emerging best practices. The pressure for productivity is not just to keep ahead of the firm across town or across the country but across the globe, where the developing capacity of potential competitors has arisen in India, China, Brazil and Eastern Europe.

In *Never Eat Alone and Other Secrets to Success One Relationship at a Time*, Keith Ferrazzi relates this important perspective about the need to manage your career in times that are changing radically:

"Branding guru and all-star business consultant Tom Peters insists that we live in a 'world turned upside down.' The conventions of the past are meaningless. Rules are irrelevant. The lines have blurred between new and old economy, Hollywood, huge corporations, and simply huge incorporated individuals.

It's what Peters calls the 'white-collar revolution.' A confluence of factors—including a streamlining of business processes, technology that replaces jobs, an increase in outsourcing to foreign countries, and an age of entrepreneurialism where more and more people see themselves as free agents—are combining in such a way that Peters predicts over 90 percent of all white-collar jobs will be radically different or won't exist at all in ten to fifteen years. He says, 'You must think of your job, your department, your division as a self-contained Inc.'"[50]

Every one of my clients is dealing with this reality in one form or another. Many of them are dealing with the many opportunities that success has dealt them, but the challenges are pushing against some of the fundamental assumptions and beliefs about their business models in very uncomfortable ways. The biggest challenge is for them to discern how to figure it all out. As the old adage goes, "many hands make light work." If you can leverage a network of folks with valuable insights, won't that help you get answers or strategies more effectively?

Ferrazzi stresses that networking is really about generosity, and I believe that is a wonderful metaphor for this critical concept. Ferrazzi says, "There's no need to ponder whether it's their lunch or yours. There's no point in keeping track of favors done and owed. Who cares? Bottom line: It's better to give before you receive. And never keep score. If your interactions are ruled by generosity, your rewards will follow suit."[51] Or as the Bible says, "A man reaps what he sows."

In my discussions with my clients over the years, I have stressed a four-step plan to reengage in the networking process or get it kick started:

1. Identify the top 40 people you know who are interesting, compelling, knowledgeable and possibly helpful to you and your organization. Look through your Outlook or Rolodex (Now that dates me!) files. You have their names in there for a reason and must have either met them or connected with them in some manner. Write down their names and phone numbers and and keep them handy. Make a promise to yourself that in the next 90 days you will try to connect with 20 of those people. That's about one every third workday. Each call may not take more than 15 minutes. It's not a lot of time for the return on the investment.

2. Think of a question or two that you would like to ask. Be prepared and make it clear that you have a quick inquiry. Have your assistant call ahead to schedule a time for a chat if that works better for you. Make the call and ask the question(s). Get ready to pick their brain! Enjoy the dialogue.

3. Try to connect with them in a personal fashion. Look up something about them before you call to show that you have invested in this effort. Use Google, the company's website, LinkedIn or other sources to find out what's going on with their company and them. Call their PR department if you need more data. What do you know about them from when you met or have found out that you can mention? Show you are interested in them.

4. Have an "elevator" speech prepared about yourself. That is three to five sentences about how things are going for you and what you are working on. It's referred to as an elevator speech because if you were asked on an elevator what you've been up to lately, you'd have only a short time to convey a message. Do not share your pain with them; don't be anything but honest, but even if things are not going well, stress the positive. So make it short, memorable, upbeat and perhaps enough to make the other person want to ask more. If they are interested, you've achieved a first step in building a relationship. If not, don't be discouraged; they may need to get to another call or meeting or they just need to think about the dialogue you've had some more. If they say they have 15 minutes, be done in 14. This may be all you need to keep the dialogue going later.

You haven't asked them for much other than their opinion and those can be short and sweet calls. The key thing is you have connected with them and put yourself in their mind's eye. This can go a long way toward beginning powerful ongoing dialogues, as perhaps they will think of you when they have questions or issues.

Introductory calls are not easy to make, but it is a matter of critical importance for you to work on establishing and maintaining this network. In terms of exploiting the value of your "brand," this process must become a regular part of your work world. As Ferrazzi so aptly summarized:

"Job security? Experience will not save you in hard times, nor will hard work or talent. If you need a job, money, advice, help, hope, or a means to make a sale, there's only one surefire, fail-safe place to find them—within your extended circle of friends and associates.

The business world is a fluid, competitive landscape; yesterday's assistant is today's influence peddler. Many of the young men and women who used to answer my phones now thankfully take my calls. Remember, it's easier to get ahead in the world when those below you are happy to help you get ahead, rather than hoping for your downfall.

Each of us is now a brand. Gone are the days where your value as an employee was linked to your loyalty and seniority. Companies use branding to develop strong, enduring relationships with customers. In today's fluid economy, you must do the same with your network.

I would argue that your relationships with others are your finest, most credible expression of who you are and what you have to offer. Nothing else compares."[52]

The process of networking effectively will require that you begin to understand through experience that building relationships really can pay off for you and for all those in your ever-expanding network. I urge everyone to make networking a critical and regular part of their work and personal lives. It's an investment that reaps substantial benefits for you, your company and all the connections in the network you develop.

Ask yourself:

- What is my attitude toward networking? Am I afraid of it, unfamiliar with it or do I know it's something I should value but have not put any effort into?

- What can I do to get started and what can I accomplish in the next 90 days?

Suggested Resources

Leadership

Coaching For Leadership: How the World's Greatest Coaches Help the Leaders Learn, Marshall Goldsmith, Laurence Lyons, Alyssa Freas, Jossey-Bass/Pfeiffer, San Francisco, CA, 2000.

Execution: The Discipline of Getting Things Done, Larry Bossidy & Ram Charan, Crown Business, New York, NY, 2002.

Good to Great, Jim Collins, Harper Collins, New York, NY, 2001.

Leaders: The Strategies for Taking Charge, The Four Keys for Effective Leadership, Warren Bennis and Burt Nanus, Wilson Learning Corporation, Eden Prairie, MN, 1985.

Overcoming the Five Dysfunctions of a Team: A Field Guide for Leaders, Managers, and Facilitators, Patrick Lencioni, Jossey-Bass, San Francisco, CA, 2005.

The Art of War, Sun Tzu, Dell Publishing, New York, New York. 1983. Edited by James Clavell.

The Coaching Revolution: How Visionary Managers Are Using Coaching to Empower People and Unlock their Full Potential, David Logan, Ph.D. and John King, Adams Media Corporation, Holbrook, MA, 2001.

The Engaging Leader: Winning with Today's Free Agent Workforce, Ed Gubman, PhD., Dearborn Trade Publishing, USA, 2003.

The Five Temptations of a CEO, A Leadership Fable, Patrick Lencioni, Jossey-Bass, San Francisco, CA, 2005.

The Leader of the Future, Frances Hesselbein, Marshal Goldsmith, The Peter Drucker Foundation, New York, NY, 1996.

The Leader of the Future 2: Visions, Strategies, and Practices for the New Era, Frances Hesselbein, Marshal Goldsmith, Jossey-Bass, San Francisco, CA, 2006.

Time

DEATH by Meeting, Patrick Lencioni, Jossey-Bass, San Francisco, CA, 2004.

First Things First, Stephen R. Covey, A. Roger Merrill, Rebecca R. Merrill, Fireside, New York, NY, 1995.

Getting Things Done: The Art of Stress-free Productivity, David Allen, Penguin Group, New York, NY, 2001.

How To Make Meetings Work, Michael Doyle and David Straus, The Berkley Publishing Group, New York, NY, 1976.

Let's Stop Meeting Like This: Tools to Save Time and Get More Done, Dick & Emily Axelrod, Berrett-Koehler Publishers, San Francisco, CA, 2014.

Ready for Anything, David Allen, Penguin Group, New York, NY, 2003.

Communications

Executive Presence: The Art of Commanding Respect Like A CEO, Harrison Monarth, McGraw Hill, New York, NY, 2010.

Powerful Conversations: How High Impact Leaders Communicate, Phil Harkins, Mc Graw-Hill, New York, NY, 1999.

Thanks for the Feedback: The Science and Art of Receiving Feedback Well, Shelia Heen and Douglas Stone, Penguin Books, New York, NY, 2014.

The Art of Woo: Using Strategic Persuasion to Sell Your Ideas, G, Richard Shell and Mario Moussa, Penguin Books, 2008.

Change

A Sense of Urgency, John P. Kotter, Harvard Business School Publishing, Boston, MA, 2008.

Leading Change, John P. Kotter, Harvard Business School Press, Boston, MA, 1996.

Managing Transitions: Making the Most of Change, William Bridges, De Capo Press Cambridge Massachusetts 2003.

The Challenge of Organizational Change: How Companies Experience It and Leaders Guide It, Rosabeth Moss Kanter, Barry A. Stein, Todd D. Jick, The Free Press, New York, NY, 1992.

The First 90 Days: Critical Success Strategies for New Leaders at All Levels, Michael Watkins, Harvard Business School Publishing, Boston, MA, 2003.

Relationships

Danger in the Comfort Zone: From Boardroom to Mailroom — How to Break the Entitlement Habit That's Killing American Business, Judith M. Bardwick, American Management Association, New York, NY, 1991.

Fiefdom Syndrome, Robert J. Herbold, Random House Inc., USA, 2004.

Give and Take: A Revolutionary Approach to Success, Adam Grant, Penguin Group, New York, NY, 2013.

Never Eat Alone: And Other Secrets to Success, One Relationship at a Time, Keith Ferrazzi with Tahl Raz. Doubleday, USA, 2005.

The Empowered Manager: Positive Political Skills at Work, Peter Block, Jossey-Bass Inc. Publishers, San Francisco, CA, 1987.

The No Asshole Rule: Building a Civilized Workplace and Surviving One That Isn't, Robert I. Sutton, PhD, Warner Business Books, New York, NY, 2007.

Too Perfect: When Being In Control Gets Out of Control, Allan E. Mallinger & Jeannette DeWyze, Fawcett Books, New York, NY, 1992.

What Got You Here Won't Get You There, Marshall Goldsmith with Mark Reiter, Hyperion, New York, NY, 2007.

Working with Emotional Intelligence, Daniel Coleman, Bantam Books, New York, NY, 1998.

ACKNOWLEDGEMENTS

I WOULD FIRST LIKE TO THANK my many clients over the years whose thirst for growth and development has fueled my enthusiasm and commitment for my work. They have also provided the examples that bring many of the models I use to life and are reflected in this book. They make me realize how blessed I have been to do this for a living.

The most important person in developing this book and in supporting my work as a leadership coach has been my wonderful assistant, Naomi Siebert. We have worked together for many years and she has always been bright, capable and supportive in all ways. She is my other face to my clients and no one has ever had anything but wonderful things to say about her style and professionalism. Her eyes were on every word of this book and my association with her has been one of the great joys of my career and life.

Zack Reboletti I have known since he was about 7. He has grown up and now runs getwebfocused.com, which delivers professional SEO and web design services. Zack has provided support and suggestions for my website and helped with my blog posting for several years, and has been invaluable.

Isidora Lagos is a friend and former client who has selflessly provided editing and moral support for this book. She's inspired me when I needed it most.

Sarah Zeffiro is the artist who created the cover art for this book. Her work can be seen on her website, www.zeffiroart.com. Sarah has a dynamic presence in the art scene in Pittsburgh through her Moving Art productions and her work has been purchased and commissioned by various collectors. I am proud to say that one of her pieces graces my living room wall.

Thanks to Kim Bookless, www.kimbookless.com, who led me through the publishing process.

AUTHOR BIOGRAPHY

WILLIAM G. STEINER is the President of Executive Coaching Concepts, a consulting firm dedicated to assisting senior executives in taking their individual and organizational performance "TO THE NEXT LEVEL." He has provided valuable counsel to senior executives throughout his career. Willy estimates that his 350-plus coaching clients in North America, Europe and Asia, in over 50 companies, have provided him a broad range of experiences that enhance his perspectives greatly. In addition, he has led hundreds more clients in seminars, presentations and speaking engagements, both in his corporate stops and in his teaching and community work.

Willy has assisted in meeting diverse organizational challenges, such as complex international mergers and divestitures, blending of distinct organizational and national cultures, and supporting growth in international markets. Willy fine-tuned his skills in leading organizational change, building high-performing teams and devising innovative incentive systems with General Electric, RCA Corp. and Galileo International. He has assisted executives in driving change by creating urgency, focus and alignment, with a keen eye for the communications implications and insights into the relationships that need to be sustained and cultivated along the way.

In addition, Willy was the President of SEI, a wholesale distributor of consumer electronics and appliances throughout the Midwest. He has a broad range of international experience and is very interested in leadership in global organizations. He holds an undergraduate degree in Economics and an MBA in Industrial Relations, both from Indiana University.

Willy is the proud father of three grown children who are successfully making their way in the world. He lives in Evanston, Illinois, just a few blocks from Lake Michigan. He is an avid golfer, storyteller, walker and reader, and he loves to travel. He writes a leadership blog every other week on his website, www.executivecoachingconcepts. com. He is active in his church and leads a monthly effort with a homeless mission. He recently took up scuba diving and is eager to explore the depths.

BIBLIOGRAPHY

1 Simon Sinek. "How Great Leaders Inspire Action: Start with Why." http://www.ted.com/talks/simon_sinek_how_great_leaders_inspire_action?language=en

2 Ken Follett. *The Edge of Eternity*. (New York, NY: The Penguin Group, 2014).

3 Peter Drucker. *The Leader of the Future* (San Francisco, CA: Jossey-Bass Publishers, 1996), pp. xii-xiii.

4 Larry Bossidy, "What Your Leader Expects of You—And What You Should Expect in Return." *Harvard Business Review*, April 2007, pp. 58-65. Accessible online at https://hbr.org/2007/04/what-your-leader-expects-of-you

5 Allan Mallinger, M.D., and Jeannette DeWyze,. *Too Perfect: When Being In Control Gets Out of Control*. (Columbine, New York: Fawcette, 1992).

6 Ibid., p. 3.

7 Ibid., p. 140.

8 Robert I Sutton, PhD, *No Asshole Rule: Building a Civilized Workplace and Surviving One That Isn't*. (New York, NY: Warner Business Books, 2007).

9 Robert I Sutton, PhD. *Good Boss, Bad Boss: How to Be the Best and Learn from the Worst*. (New York, NY: Business Plus, 2012).

10 Sutton. *No Asshole Rule*, pp. 124-126.

11 Sutton. *No Asshole Rule*, pp. 136-154.

12 Ed Gubman. *The Engaging Leader: Winning with Today's Free Agent Workforce*. (Chicago, IL: Dearborn Trade Publishing, 2003).

13 Marshall Goldsmith. *What Got You Here Won't Get You There*. (New York,

NY: 2007).

14 Joe Martino. "Top Five Regrets of the Dying," Collective Evolution, Based on Bonnie Ware. *The Top Five Regrets of the Dying: A Life Transformed by the Dearly Departing.* (Carlsbad, CA: Hay House, Inc., 2011). Posted: 08/03/2013. http://www.collective-evolution.com/2013/04/27/the-top-5-regrets-of-the-dying/

15 Marshall Goldsmith. "The One Question You Need to Ask Yourself before You Say Anything," Posted February 9, 2015. http://www.marshallgoldsmithfeedforward.com/marshallgoldsmithblog/?p=852

16 Rachel Emma Silverman and Nikki Waller. "The Algorithm That Tells the Boss Who Might Quit," *The Wall Street Journal*, March 13, 2015. http://www.wsj.com/articles/the-algorithm-that-tells-the-boss-who-might-quit-1426287935

17 Adam Grant. *Give and Take: A Revolutionary Approach to Success.* (New York; NY: Penguin Group, 2013).

18 Russell Bishop. *Workarounds That Work: How to Conquer Anything That Stands in Your Way at Work.* (New York, NY: McGraw Hill, 2011). pp. 22, 35.

19 Bruce Tulgan. "The Under-management Epidemic Report 2014: Ten Years Later." http://rainmakerthinking.com/wp-management-epidemic-report-2014-ten-years-later/

20 Stephen Covey. *First Things First.* (New York, NY: Simon and Schuster, 1994).

21 Mitch Albom. *Tuesday's with Morrie.* (New York, NY: Doubleday, 1997), pp.135-136.

22 Marshall Goldsmith. "The Skill That Separates," *Fast Company*, July 2005. Accessible at http://www.marshallgoldsmithlibrary.com/cim/articles_display.php?aid=270

23 Randy Pausch and Jeffrey Zaslow. *The Last Lecture.* (New York, NY: Hyperion, 2008), p. 162.

24 Elaina Zuker. *Mastering Assertiveness Skills.* (New York, NY: Amacom, American Management Association, 1983), p.63.

25 Thomas Gordon. *Leadership Effectiveness Training.* (New York, NY: The Berkley Publishing Group, 1977).

26 Adapted from Phil Harkins, *Powerful Conversations: How High Impact Leaders Communicate.* (New York, NY: McGraw Hill, 1999), pp. 63-64.

27 Michael Moffa. "The Danger of Joking at Work: The Rise and Fall of Workplace Humor," February 7, 2012. https://www.recruiter.com/i/joking-at-work/

28 Clive Thompson. "End the Tyranny of 24/7 Email." *The New York Times,* August 28, 2014. http://www.nytimes.com/2014/08/29/opinion/end-the-tyranny-of-24-7-mail.html?smid=nytcore-iphone-share&smprod=nyt-core-iphone

29 Eviatar Zerubavel. *The Elephant in the Room: Silence and Denial in Everyday Life.* (Oxford, England: Oxford University Press, 2006).

30 Michael Watkins. *The First 90 Days: Critical Success Strategies for New Leaders at All Levels.* (Boston, MA: Harvard Business School Press, 2003).

31 Adapted from William Bridges. *Managing Transitions: Making the Most of Change.* (Cambridge, MA: DaCapo Press, 2003).

32 Alan Deutschman. "Change or Die," *Fast Company*, May 1, 2005, pp. 52-62.

33 Gregory P. Shea, PhD, and Cassie Solomon. "The Year of M&A? Beating the Odds of Failure." CNBC Guest Author Blog, Monday, February 25, 2013. Accessible at http://www.cnbc.com/id/100485912

34 William Bridges. "The Three Questions," Copyright 2009, William Bridges and Associates.

35 William Bridges. *Managing Transitions: Making the Most of Change.* (Cambridge, MA: DaCapo Press, 2003).

36 Peter Block. *The Empowered Manager: Positive Political Skills at Work.* (San Francisco, CA: Josey-Bass Publishers, 1987), pp. 137-160.

37 Bruce Tulgan. "Pent-Up Departure Demand: The Swelling Ranks of Employees Who Would Leave if They Could," *Just Thinking*, March 14, 2014. http://rainmakerthinking.com/newsletters/pent-departure-demand/

38 Phil Jackson. *11 Rings: The Soul of Success*. (New York, NY: Penguin Books, 2013).

39 Phil Jackson. *Sacred Hoops*. (New York, NY: Hyperion Press, NY, 1995), p. 135.

40 Eric Berne. *Games People Play*. (New York, NY: Ballantine Books, 1964). Material adapted from the International Transactional Analysis Association (ITAA). See https:/itaaworld.org/what-transactional-analysis.

41 Roman Krznaric, "Six Habits of Highly Empathic People," *Greater Good online newsletter*. Nov 27, 2012. http://greatergood.berkeley.edu/article/item/six_habits_of_highly_empathic_people1

42 Jeff Immelt. "Things Leaders Do," *Fast Company*, April 1, 2004, p. 57.

43 Marshall Goldsmith: *What Got You Here Won't Get You There*. (New York, NY: Hyperion, 2007).

44 Allan E. Mallinger, M.D., and Jeanette DeWyze. *Too Perfect: When Being In Control Gets Out of Control*. (New York, NY: The Randon House Publishing Group, 1992).

45 Marshall Goldsmith. http://www.marshallgoldsmithfeedforward.com/marshallgoldsmithblog/?p=238

46 Thomas A Harris. *I'm Ok, You're Ok*. (New York, NY: Harper & Row, 1969).

47 Elaina Zuker. *Mastering Assertiveness Skills: Power and Positive Influence at Work*. (New York, NY: AMACOM Books, 1983).

48 Adam Grant. *Give and Take: A Revolutionary Approach to Success*. (New York, NY: Penguin Group, 2013).

49 http://www.mindtools.com/pages/article/newLDR_86.htm#sthash.S4E-9DrvA.dpuf

50 Keith Ferrazzi, with Tahil Raz. *Never Eat Alone and Other Secrets to Success One Relationship at a Time*. (New York, NY: Currency Books, 2005.) p. 225.

51 Ibid., pp. 174-175

52 Ibid., pp. 21-22.

10633060R00181

Made in the USA
Lexington, KY
26 September 2018